Montpelier!

Thank you for your support!

S Conway

What the Farm?

Poignant & Profane Stories
from My Unplanned Life

by

Mary Conway Sullivan

For *my husband, Sean AKA: The Dreamer, Farmer Brown, Mr. Outdoors, Moonbeam, Tiny House Tim, Bird Man, Father of the Year, Quick Draw McGraw, Captain Fun, Dr. Doolittle. Your vision made all this happen. Love you!*

Also for my mother, whose love for language, stories, and laughter lives in me and in this book.

Contents

SUMMER

THE BEAUTIFUL MUNDANE: SEASONLESS STORIES

RECIPES

Foreword

I am one of those people who really enjoys a predictable routine ...
until I don't.

There was a time in my adolescence and young adulthood when I
often felt compelled to step out of my comfort zone: get certified in
SCUBA despite my ability to get seasick in a bathtub; have a very,
very short stint in an ill-fated improv group; take a hip hop dance
class as a young mom. Nothing monumental, dangerous, or all that
thrill-seeking. But a break from the ordinary brought me a tiny bit of
personal growth ... or at least some shits, giggles, and good stories.

Once my husband and I started a family, I found my madcap muse
was getting muffled. (In my defense, what's a bigger leap out of one's
comfort zone than birthing and raising children?) I continued with
my dance classes, freelance writing, and nonprofit work, but the
energy spent seeking breaks from the ordinary lessened as I found
myself supporting my three daughters' great leaps. It was inspiring
to see them take chances, great and small, but it also made me a tiny
bit sad. "Am I done growing? I feel boring," I would catch myself
thinking.

Right about that same time, my husband, a dreamer, pushed me out
of my comfort zone big time. I had just sent my oldest daughter to
college, buried my mother after helping her through ten years of
living with Alzheimer's Disease, and put down our beloved dog. I
was catching my breath, ready to pull in my focus. With two more
daughters getting ready to go off to college and a new puppy in the
mix, I was trying to figure out what I wanted for myself. Who would I
be in this new stage of life if not a caregiver and a mother?

Then, this opportunity to purchase a farm fell into our laps. Once we
saw the property on that crisp, beautiful October day, my husband
got a look of enchantment in his eyes. I remember sitting in my
car back then, after we had purchased the farm, weepily explaining
to my sister, Susan, that I felt like I was being railroaded into <u>his</u>
dream. I hadn't even taken the time to figure out what my dream was.

Frankly, I resented him for dreaming first. Where was <u>my</u> daring? <u>My</u> dreaming? I felt like a follower.

Looking back on that time now, I feel so silly, bratty, and indulged. How was I to know that Susan would—about a year later—whisper to me and my other sisters that she was in the throes of early onset Alzheimer's Disease. Surely, she knew or at least suspected it when I talked to her that day about my misgivings about the farm.

I had no idea then that our farm was to become a haven, an inland island of retreat for Susan as she declined into Alzheimer's Disease. Over the course of the ensuing decade, it became a sanctuary for her and several other family members who were experiencing illness, death and dying. My own nuclear family found the healing that nature brings as we all recovered from feeling depleted, retreating to the farm to be alone (or together). And we hunkered down there during the Great Shutdown of 2020. What a blessing this farm has turned out to be.

What follows is a collection of essays that chronicle the first several years of my farm adventure. Some stories are silly; others are contemplative. And some are examples of me learning the difference between life in my full-time home in Northeast Ohio vs. a part-time life on a farm. To be clear, I am still a farm poser. But I'm so grateful for the inspirational and enlightening happenings that this surprising chapter of my life has brought me and my family. I hope you enjoy reading this as much as I have enjoyed living it and chronicling it.

Introduction: Listen, I'm Not Amish

"I just want to stop and look at this farm while we're out," he said.

"Oh, for chrissakes," I thought. I had been down this road before.

Several years prior, my husband had brought me and my three daughters to a godforsaken, wouldn't-hit-a-dog-in-the-ass-with-it, muddy, lumpy farm in northern/mid-Ohio. At the time, he desperately wanted a goat farm.

"We should get ahead of this growing market. Goat meat is the fastest growing protein in the country. We could raise goats. Get a jump on the competition, corner the market, be the goat gods," he told me.

So, there we were, trudging through another desolate property. The girls were dizzy with the prospect of owning a farm, shouting out ebullient phrases like, "Dad, can I get a puppy on the farm?!" or "Can I get a pig, Dad?! " or "Ducklings! Ooooo. Ducklings, Dad!"

"Um .... wait. We're just looking, everyone. Slow down," I said.

Later that night, I put three ecstatic little girls to bed, visions of farm animals dancing in their heads. I sat down next to my husband, looked him straight in the eyes, and spoke my truth: "Sweetheart, I get it. Farms are cool. But they are a lot of work. All I see in this fantasy is work for me. Me. Not you. "

You see, my husband is an entrepreneur, and he's an expert at delegating. He's the original Tom Sawyer. I could just see me mucking stalls and wiping my brow like a Dust Bowl era heroine while he would breeze in and out of "the farm," carefree and happy.

I started to gather steam. "So, we're going to move from our suburban home to be ... what? Farmers? We don't know anything about farms or farming. Maybe we should start with you pulling a weed or two here at our suburban home. You don't even cut the grass, for God's sake."

The glimmer went out of his eyes.

I continued, "You and your next Amish wife will be very happy together. Knock yourself out. God bless. I'm out."

Ten years later, we bought a farm.

AUTUMN

Amish Guys Got Swagger

I begrudgingly agreed to my husband's farm fantasy after ten years of his begging. I don't know how it happened, really. We stopped in to look at a farm one day in 2010. It was one of those magical autumn days in Ohio. As we drove through the gates, rather than seeing steaming piles of God knows what, I saw rolling, grassy, well-manicured hills and horses frolicking about. The air was crisp and cool. The sun shimmered on the yellow and orange leaves of the trees. It was breathtaking.

"Okay," I thought, "You've got my attention."

A four-wheeler tour of the property, a glass of wine, and an al fresco lunch of locally-raised pork with salad greens right from the garden … some bids and counter bids and … boom! We were farm owners. Well, we were weekend farm owners, really. Like posers. Because we wanted to stay married, we kept our suburban house. This farm fantasy would only work because it was actually a self-sufficient, well-run business.

So, just as I was entering a crossroads in my life, ready to clean out junk drawers in my kitchen and maybe find my "calling" in there, I found myself making plans to build a farmhouse. My husband, "Farmer Brown," and I are both from very large families. This adventure would only be fun if we had playmates, so we had a house built that could hold a sizable group of folks for dinner (and a lot of beds because our friends and family like wine). We interviewed various builders of all stripes, and in the end, we chose the Amish guy. Not because he was the cheapest, but quite frankly, because the guy had swagger. He wasn't allowed to have zippers or a belt, but dang, he had swagger.

The Amish guy was actually one of a dynamic duo of brothers, Levi and Uriah. I didn't know much about the ins and outs of the Amish lifestyle before this, but I was expecting much quainter, country bumpkin fellows. Not at all the case, as it turned out. Tall, lanky, and bearded, Levi was the father of nine boys. I'm one of nine, so we had some simpatico. Uriah, or Uri, was the office guy. He was very efficient—showing samples of beautiful wood; going over blueprints and roofing materials; and closing the deal. Only his bowl haircut gave a hint that he was Amish. I was kind of like, "Are you putting me on? Are you really Amish or is there a Jag out back and scotch in your bottom drawer?" He was legit, though.

Levi was the day-to-day on-site guy. He had his own driver—a fine "English"(non-Amish) man who drove him everywhere he needed to go because the Amish don't drive cars. They call them "Yoder Toters" out there. When he would arrive for our weekly meetings, he'd amble out of the truck like an underdressed rock star and saunter over to me, a toothpick in his mouth. He had a glint in his eye that said, "Yeah, I'm rocking these overalls and straw hat, lady." And he did. A handsome devil, I have to say. Not exactly Harrison Ford in *Witness*, but kind of an Amish Michael Keaton, if that makes any sense.

It was hard to know the rules of these Amish folks. Levi didn't drive, but he and Uri did both have email addresses and cell phones. When I visited their Amish cabinet maker in the remote back hills of Ohio, his office was steamy—no air conditioning in 100-degree heat—located in a barn with a gaslight hanging from the ceiling … over a desktop computer. Talk about a culture clash.

I got comfortable with Levi after a few weeks. When things looked like they were slowing down, I'd playfully punch him in the shoulder, "We're going to be in by Thanksgiving; right, Levi?"

"Oh yeah, Miss Mary, we'll be done by then," he would cockily reply.

I liked the guy, so I hoped he wasn't lying. (My husband is an entrepreneur who doesn't take BS from anyone, not even a handsome Amish housing magnate.) He had a stopwatch going. One bearded man against another, and my husband was clearly not intimidated by that straw hat.

Uri and Levi were true to their word, and, as the deadline loomed, a flurry of silent, hardworking, task-driven Amish craftsmen descended on the property. They had that darned house built in eight months' time, and we were sitting down to Thanksgiving dinner, right on schedule.

Spiders, Man!

My husband, "Mr. Outdoors," loves spiders. All throughout our marriage and raising our kids, he forbade any of us from killing house spiders. "They're good luck," he'd say. "They eat bugs. Let them be." And for the most part, we complied.

The majority of the time, we live away from the farm, very close to Lake Erie where there are large lake spiders. Spider webs are beautiful, fascinating works of art, really. The way they appear out of nowhere in the morning, the dew glistening on them in the sunlight, is downright magical. These Lake Erie spiders are always busy catching mosquitoes and midges. They're needed and appreciated.

The spiders that really creep me out are those that roam around, the "hunters."

On a warm Indian Summer day at the very start of fall, my daughter, Ginny, and I got to the farm and excitedly got our swimsuits on for a dip in the pool. We retracted the pool cover and prepared to jump in. "Holy crap, there are spiders!" she screamed. "Lots of them."

There, lining the sides of the pool and—I am not lying here—walking on top of the water and swimming in the water, were about a dozen huge, muzzy black spiders. I immediately called our farm manager, Mark, for help (I call Mark "The Sheriff," because he's in charge of all the things). He knows everything about everything and was afraid of nothing. Or so I thought. He replied to my pleas for help with an unhelpful, "I don't do spiders. They creep me out. I'll send someone over."

It made me think of that scene from *Raiders of the Lost Ark* when Harrison Ford says, "Snakes. Why'd it have to be snakes?" We all, it seems, have our weaknesses.

As Ginny and I cowered in the corner, "The Sheriff's" strapping son came over in his t-shirt and jeans to patiently scoop up the spiders and squish them with his big cowboy boots. "Yeah, we get these at this time of year," he explained, calmly dipping the pool skimming net into the water. "They're called field wolf spiders. Once it starts getting chilly, they come up from the fields looking for the warmth of the pool at night."

That image grossed me out even more. I pictured legions of spiders marching toward our house, invading at night while we naively slept inside. "Thanks for the nightmare fuel," I scoffed.

Some spiders were back the next morning, so I put on my big girl underpants, swallowed hard, then began scooping and squashing those bastards like it was my job. I was quite proud of myself. "I mean, I'm a sometimes-y farm girl," I told myself. "I got this."

The following week, I went to the farm for one last Indian Summer swim and to join my husband, who was already there. "I can't wait to jump in that pool," I said to the dog as we drove in. I didn't give the spiders from the previous week a second thought. First, I had to clear off the pool deck, so I grabbed the leaf blower to get debris off the pool cover and patio. "Oh darn, it looks like we left the pool rafts out from last week," I said, still chatting with the dog. I turned the leaf blower toward the stack of rafts and pool noodles in the corner. What happened next was like a scene from a scary movie.

The spiders were back. And they had multiplied … big time. Dozens and dozens of black, muzzy, humongous spiders skittered. All. Over. The. Deck. It was like special effects from a horror movie, like they were CGI animation. They seemed to just keep coming. Everywhere. An otherworldly scream came out of my mouth that I don't remember ever hearing before. The dog took off, creeped out by the spiders, too. Or my screaming. Or both.

I tried to squash some of them, but they outnumbered me so much, I just couldn't keep up. I was totally losing it, becoming more and more unglued by the second.

Pretty soon, "Mr. Outdoors" showed up. He'd been walking the property and heard my screams from afar. "What the hell is going on?" he yelled as he approached, eyeing the dog that was still cowering around the corner of the house.

"There are spiders everywhere. Do something!" I screamed tearfully. "And don't even start with that 'they're good luck' bullshit."

I retreated to the pool to tread water and monitor as he dutifully killed the invading army of arachnids. "Wow," I said to myself, trying to keep away from the spidery sides of the pool. "He must really love me. He's killing spiders. For me." Thirty years into our marriage, he had chosen me over spiders. It was progress.

Please Pass the Percocet

It was all set to be a picture-perfect holiday in our new farmhouse …
until I sent my daughters on a drug run from the dinner table.

Our gorgeous farm table was beautifully set with crisp, white
plates; darling mason jar water glasses; and colorful leaves from the
surrounding woods dotting the table. Dim lights and candles plus
a tasty locally-raised turkey roasting in the spanking new oven. My
husband was right. This was the greatest decision in our marriage:
being sometimes-y farmers.

Filled with fresh air and holiday zeal, I had started Thanksgiving Day
with a hike and yoga with my daughters. I thought that keeping busy
would take my mind off the dull, thumping pain in my mouth.

"No worries," I thought. "Just focus on the Thanksgiving Day Parade,
The National Dog Show, and peeling potatoes."

Hours later, my in-laws arrived and were appropriately wowed by the
beautiful tablescape and kitchen aromas.

We all sat down and began The Thanksgiving Feed.

And then: "Why am I having labor pains in my mouth?" I thought to
myself after my first bite of turkey. One of my molars had been giving
me problems for months, but all of a sudden, something felt different
… ominous.

As the blinding, thumping, unspeakable pain jolted through my
jaw and head, and I let out a string of ugly expletives in front of my
mother-in-law that would make Nicki Minaj blush. The poor thing
was surely thinking, "Do we need to call an exorcist?"

I took to the bed. Ice packs, moaning, more nasty toads jumping out of my mouth. I popped Advil and Tylenol like Halloween candy. Nothing was touching this pain. I mean, I have gone through labor three times with large-headed children. This pain was way, way beyond that.

I sent an SOS to my dentist pleading, begging, for help. For drugs, quite frankly. But, unfortunately, we were in small-town Ohio on a holiday. And there were no pharmacies open in a two-hour radius. I fell into a sad, pathetic lump, when a miracle happened. Not only did my dentist call me back, but he and my daughters orchestrated a holiday drug drop for me.

Saint Dentist left his family's Thanksgiving table to bring me an emergency supply of prescription painkillers. They were to meet him halfway at a truck stop off the highway. As my daughters scurried out the door, I pushed a pumpkin pie and a bottle of wine into their hands to give him as thanks. I didn't know what the etiquette on that kind of thing was, but it was all I could think of in my blinding pain.

My daughters were Thanksgiving drug mules and came back to the farm with just enough Percocet to shush the pain.

I finally fell into a misty, drug-induced sleep, the sounds of dishes and the hushed, shocked mumblings of my in-laws ringing in my ears. The toads were safely back inside my mouth. I spent the next day in a haze as we hosted about 100 family members with hayrides, leftovers, and a roaring fire.

While it wasn't the Thanksgiving I had planned for the previous seven months, there were many blessings at that table.

First of all, we were sitting in a beautiful house that was finished just in the nick of time thanks to my husband breathing down my neck and haranguing the Amish builders. Then there was the meal itself.

I can't vouch for how it tasted, as I was incapacitated by pain, but it looked and smelled amazing. My people were tucked in safely around me. And there was the miracle of Saint Dentist; the expediency of our daughters, Ginny and Rose; and the blessing of modern pharmaceuticals. And we had established a new tradition: The Farm Thanksgiving.

On Walking

I've always been a walker. I guess I got it from my dad. He loved to go for walks after dinner, and I would often accompany him when I was little—my shorter legs taking four steps for every one of his long, six-foot-four-inch-tall strides.

My body just doesn't like running. I would sooner walk from here to the moon than go for a run from here to the corner. For me, walking is exercise, meditation, prayer, and therapy all rolled into one.

Part of our routine on the farm is to take long walks through the woods, up one hill, down another. We pass cornfields, yearling horses, mooing cows, and babbling creeks. Sherrie, the wife of the former owner of the property, was an avid walker like me. I'd see her making her daily seven-mile loop as I would drive in. I could tell she found the same therapy in it that I do. Sherrie left us too soon, dying suddenly just a couple of years after we purchased the farm. I guess God wanted to show her even better trails, but I think of her with her sunny smile and friendly wave every time I walk the property.

Just after we acquired the farm property, I had a chance to take an epic walk with friends: El Camino de Santiago de Compostela in Spain. I had heard of this centuries-old pilgrimage—the Way of St. James—years ago from my college roommate. The entire Camino is some 400 miles and stretches from the southern border of France, over the Pyrenees Mountains, and across the top of Spain to Santiago (the supposed burial site of St. James).

The thing I loved most about El Camino was the slowing down, the simple enjoyment of the journey itself. I fondly recall a day when I found myself walking alone across the countryside, my Camino companions scattered ahead and behind me. I was listening to the breeze through the trees and the sounds of lonesome cowbells. The simple serenity was so peaceful. All that day I sent up silent prayers to my recently-deceased mother for a sign that all was well. Just when

I thought my prayers weren't being heard, I came across her name—Marge—scrawled across a bridge overpass that I was walking under. It took my breath away, making me laugh and cry at the same time because it was so my mom: not subtle at all.

Later on, we had the opportunity to visit a Michelin-starred restaurant in San Sebastián, Spain. We were underdressed in our practical, Lands' End travel dresses. The meal was a journey in itself: a culinary parade of amuse bouche, coulis, en glace this or that, followed by a pastiche of foamy things, free-range fungi, and closing with an artisanal plate of local queso. Oh and there was lots of wine, chosen purely by running a finger down the menu to find the wine with the least amount of digits next to it.

As the meal went on, we all got church giggles from trying so hard to be as pretentious as the menu. To stifle myself, I fled to the bathroom to splash water on my face, giggling into the sink. I took a deep breath, smoothed my dress, and started to head back out to behave like a grown up. But then I spied a glistening glass container full of disposable toothbrushes because I guess pretentious diners have impeccable dental hygiene. Emboldened by the wine, I grabbed a fistful of toothbrushes, shoving them into my fanny pack and tripping back to the table, tears of laughter streaming down my face. At that same moment, the stylish manager, Carmen, dressed in a well-appointed black-on-black ensemble that was decidedly *not* a travel dress, came over to the table. "Did everyone enjoy their meal?" she asked mysteriously as a hush fell on the table.

I swallowed hard. "Oh good God," I thought. "She knows I stole those toothbrushes. I am so busted."

"I would ask you to please follow me," Carmen said, turning on her heel.

"Oh shit," I said under my breath. "I think I just got us arrested." I brainstormed how to explain my incarceration to my husband. My Camino mates fell into an uneasy silence.

Carmen then walked us all into the kitchen, where I looked around for the local Spanish Guardia waiting to whisk me away. But all that was there were the chefs and cooks, ready to give us a private tour. My friend, Gretchen, forgot that she had planned a behind-the-scenes tour of this famous restaurant. My travel companions and I all laughed uncontrollably with relief. I was never so happy to be free.

Walking further, a small group of my Camino travelers found ourselves just outside of San Sebastián, where we stumbled into an impromptu private Mass in the home of St. Ignatius of Loyola. We arrived at the site about a half hour before closing, so we hurriedly toured the house and found ourselves on the third floor. I poked around curiously and came upon a little chapel there, built in the same room where St. Ignatius is said to have had his conversion. "We are just about to begin Mass," a kindly priest named Gaston said to me, as he carefully set up the altar. "Please join me."

"Oh, I don't know ..." I mumbled, looking around to see if anyone else was attending the Mass. No one else was in the small, hidden chapel. After I recruited my three companions, we settled in for Mass. Because there were just us four and Father Gaston, he invited us to come and celebrate Mass on the tiny altar with him. At first, our small clutch was ruffled at the unexpectedness of this intimate Mass. And we just could not stop giggling that the priest's name was Gaston, thinking of *Disney's Beauty and the Beast* the whole time. But as the Mass proceeded in Spanish, and I interpreted what I could, I found myself overcome at how lovely, holy, and special it all was.

When it came time for petitions during Mass, we each whispered painful burdens we were carrying with us on the Camino. Kathy had just lost her mom to a sudden stroke and was still reeling from that loss. Gretchen was at a spiritual crossroads, just beginning her studies in Ignatius's *Spiritual Exercises*. Our tour guide, Sol—a glamorous Spaniard who was a ringer for Carla Bruni—choked out a request to Father Gaston to pray for her, that she had lost her faith and she was in turmoil. She had named her only son Ignacio after St. Ignatius, and she didn't know how she had gotten so far from her faith. As she confided in us all, I translated in a whisper, as if I was betraying her secret. When it was my turn to bring petitions to the altar, I shared desperate, fervent prayers for my sister Susan, who had recently been diagnosed with early onset Alzheimer's Disease, and more prayers for my sister Kathy, who had recently been diagnosed with Parkinson's Disease. "Help them, and help me help them," I begged Gaston … and God.

At the end of the Mass, as a ray of sunlight inexplicably shone through a small window, casting a supernatural light on the room, the four of us were emotionally spent and, at the same time, filled with the presence of God, and the Holy Spirit, the humility and empowerment of sharing this intimate moment. Then, from Father Gaston, "Would you like to take your picture with me? A selfie? Yes?"

As I wiped my tears away, I said, "Um … sure. Gracias, Gaston," as I posed, arm around him, as if we were drinking buddies. Well, we did share that wine …

It's good to go away. It's good to come home. Whenever I return from Camino, now having been 4 times, visions of long walks, tapas, and wine fill my daydreams for several weeks. Each time I go, it seems that I miss a wedding, a shower, a funeral, some milestone. Life and death keep coming. All of it only reinforces in me the importance of cherishing my walks, be they around the neighborhood, at the farm, or on far-flung paths. When I'm faced with the inevitable obstacles to happiness, fulfillment, and peace, I keep visualizing those walks. And I walk on in search of my own faith, meaning, inspiration, sanity, and hope.

Prairie Peddler

After a winding drive over and through hills of cornfields, we arrived. My nieces had convinced me to join them at the Prairie Peddler Festival, which, it turned out, was not located on the prairie at all, but in the woods. It was a maze of over 200 permanent structures. I joined the throng of shuffling festivalgoers buying handmade this or that and, per usual, immediately lost my husband.

My husband has a reputation for going rogue in these settings. He's very distractible. If he catches a scent of something that interests him, off he goes. I often refer to him as "Moonbeam," as in *The Sound of Music*'s "How do you hold a moonbeam in your hand?"

I was impressed that he came at all because he's not into "themed" events. I finally found him, rolling his eyes at a scarecrow that was "entertaining" passersby, occasionally coming to life and freaking out small children and old people. When we passed a couple holding hands and wearing matching red T-shirts, one reading O-H, the other reading I-O, I warily glanced over at Moonbeam. "You ok?"

Moonbeam lasted an hour, escaping to go back to our farm and do "important things" like sit on his rocking chair and survey his view. The rest of us pushed on, in search of what was being promised to me as "the best thing you'll ever taste" by my nieces.

Our group kept losing each other in the sea of flannel and blue jeans, constantly calling each other's cell phones for directions on how to find one another. It was like a party game.

"I'm at the booth with the yellow mums in front of it," my daughter explained.

I looked around, "This place is littered with mums."

"Okay, we're right next to the booth with the witches and pumpkins," she tried.

"Those are everywhere too!" I sighed.

"Okay, look for the American flag and a man dressed like Ye Olde Prairie Guy."

"There are at least 900 of those," I replied. "You're killing me."

We miraculously all reunited, spying each other somewhere between the loom demonstration and the candle dipper. We continued on together, dawdling through more booths of furniture, coconut shell lamps, and a whole genre of stuff called "primitives." I watched my daughter, nieces, and nephew peruse items for their respective homes. Then it hit me. When did they all grow out of wearing scarves from my mother's dress-up box and become funny, smart, interesting humans with jobs and houses of their own? And how is it my nieces now have children? Aren't they still children? Aren't I still a child?

As I pondered that (and whether or not I needed a coconut shell lamp), we came upon the food we were seeking. The line was long in front of the booth, everyone shuffling impatiently, looking with anticipation at the coveted steaming bowls ahead. Finally, there it was: a Styrofoam cup of piping-hot chicken noodle soup on top of mashed potatoes with —wait for it—biscuits on the side. It made my pants hurt just looking at it. "Are we preparing to run a marathon or something?" I thought.

"This is my favorite part," Lauren cooed as she cuddled the Styrofoam, blowing on its hot contents. "It's so delicious …"

I took a bite of her serving. "Hmm. It's ok," I thought. Then, a bite of my other niece, Maura's, serving. "Okay, it's nice and warm. I'll give you that." Then a bite of my nephew, Sean's, serving. Then, I just let it happen: I snarfed down a couple rounds of samples from each of them, because calories don't count when you're eating from someone else's bowl.

While the soup didn't live up to the hype, the company more than made up for it. In a sprawling, large Irish Catholic family of 30 grandchildren and 40+ great grandchildren (honestly, I'm losing count), I really enjoy having some one-on-one time. But if I do make it to another Prairie Peddler Festival, I'll remember to wear my stretchy pants.

Let It Burn

There's a ritual out in the country that fascinates me. Several times a year, farmers will round up their stuff and stack it together in a huge pile: boxes, pallets, broken furniture, and miscellaneous other stuff that accumulates in remote corners of these wide, open spaces. Then, when the wind and the humidity is just right, they will set it on fire and just burn it away.

It reminds me of when we used to burn leaf piles in the fall when I was little. While the scent was warm and earthy, someone along the line discovered it was actually bad for the air quality, and it was made illegal in our town.

But out in the country, I guess it's still legal. And that signature scent brings back all sorts of memories. Watching a huge pile burning recently, I resisted the urge to get marshmallows and chocolate for s'mores and instead gazed at the rising flames and smoke, wafting into the fading light of the early evening. It got me thinking … wouldn't it be great if I could put all my metaphorical life garbage in a pile, burn it, and go on, unencumbered and lighter?

The first thing I would put on the burn pile is Regret. I would have done things differently as a young mom, knowing what I know now. I could have been a wildly successful freelance writer if I had put myself out there more and sooner. I should have been braver and insisted on majoring in theatre, despite my father's protestations. But it can't be about the "woulda, coulda, shoulda"s. As one of my favorite yoga teachers taught me, a better mantra is, "I am here now in this." So with that, Regret, you are ashes.

The next thing I would throw on that pile is Worry: the incessant refrain of "Is everything and everyone okay? I've learned that worry doesn't help anyone and can actually do harm to me by interrupting my sleep, making me run down and giving me worry lines. A better idea is to hand it over. My father used to get angry when we would worry. "Where is your faith?!" he would ask. When I was going through some especially hard times when my kids were young and my mother was ailing, I would feel overwhelmed, hopeless, drowning in worry … until I remembered my father's advice, handed it over, and "burned it." I sent my fears and worries up to God to handle, at least for a few minutes. Whenever I was wise and faith-filled enough to do that, miracles happened. Special people would come into my life and turn the tide of worry. It was remarkable, really. So, Worry, I burn you.

That old standby, Resentment, would have to go on that pile, too. Like everyone else, I've been hurt. In setting a torch to Resentment, I release bitterness and hurt and, in the rising smoke, I feel forgiveness and freedom. Resentment is a heavy burden to carry around. I pick it up again every now and then, maybe just to remember how heavy it feels. But that sucker belongs on the burn pile. Life is too short to carry that crap around. Burn Resentment down.

Just to keep the fire burning, I'd throw a big log of Self-loathing on there. The other day, I was excitedly getting ready for a fancy gala to honor my beloved aunt-in-law when, much to my horror and surprise, I discovered that four of the five dresses I tried on were just a little too tight. One by one, I peeled them off my fleshy body as my disgust and self-loathing started to rise. Then, I started hating on myself for hating myself. "What the hell is wrong with me?" I thought. "I'm bigger than this!" (about a size bigger). For the love of God, I am too damned menopausal, hot, and tired to care about sizes and all that crap. Self-loathing, I am pouring kerosene on you to make sure you go up in smoke.

And so, while large burn piles are no longer legal in the city or suburbs, I invite all who read this to have a little metaphorical burn pile. We can all write our life garbage on little pieces of paper and burn them in our fireplaces or backyard fire pits. I've found that autumn is the perfect time to clear out the BS and to make room for gratitude. Plus, autumn is a great time of year for s'mores.

Worst Job Ever

Folks come from far and wide to enlist the expertise of the knowledgeable staff who run and manage our farm. They all have excellent reputations in their field. The horses that come to our farm to breed are impregnated through artificial insemination, as are all standardbred racehorses. (Thoroughbred horses are bred "live cover," meaning that the action is real, live, fur-to-fur.) Either way, the time-honored practice of a Teaser Horse is used. And the Teaser definitely has the worst job in the world.

When breeding a female horse, it's important to know when she's ovulating and ready to go. Nowadays, there are sophisticated means of finding that out through ultrasounds and such, but the old school way is to enlist the help of a Teaser. We have a Teaser on our farm. To protect his identity, I'll call him "Mr. Blue". When it comes time to see if a mare is ready to breed, poor Mr. Blue is invited into a stall to meet the pretty young thing. He saunters up to her, tentatively introduces himself, and gives her a sniff, all under the watchful eye of our learned farm manager, Mark. If the mare isn't feeling it, she gets aggressive and starts wailing on Mr. Blue, biting and even sometimes kicking him. "So … that's a no, then?" he mumbles.

Our farm manager, Mark then escorts a disappointed, shocked and slightly bruised Mr. Blue to the door. That's bad enough, right? Mr. Blue is like a shot-down young lad at a bar. But, it gets worse.

When the timing is right and Miss Thing, the mare, is feeling it, things get really bad. Mr. Blue is escorted in with a jaunty step as if he's wearing an ascot and smoking jacket. He approaches Miss Thing, "Hey, baby. I notice that you smell especially fine today. How about a roll in the hay?"

If Miss Thing is in the mood for love, she shows it in fine fashion, raising her tail to reveal her nether regions whilst taking a long, hot piss. Sexy stuff. Mr. Blue nods his head, "That's what I'm talking about

…" And then he is swiftly removed from the stall because Mr. Blue's semen ain't got game. His guys are not invited to Miss Thing's party.

The next scene is pretty unromantic. Mark quietly enters the stall, whispers sweet nothings into Miss Thing's ears, whips out the turkey baster, and efficiently inseminates her with some prize-winning stuff, using some very, very long rubber gloves.

Mr. Blue goes back to his lonely stall. But Mark and his staff are good to Mr. Blue. They make sure he feels the love from them, but I'm afraid it's just not the same.

When I expressed concern about Mr. Blue's repeatedly broken heart, Mark assured me that Mr. Blue "takes care of himself, not to worry." My mind reels trying to figure out what that means.

Shortly after we acquired the farm, I was walking through the barn with my youngest daughter, Rose, who was then 14-years-old and a freshman in high school. When we came upon Mr. Blue, I petted his nose and whispered empathetically, "Hello, Mr. Teaser."

"Mom, what's a Teaser?" she asked. As I explained to her the details above, she listened intently, nodding wide-eyed, mouth agape. She then let out a long exhale and looked at me hard. "So," she finally said quietly, "The Teaser is in the 'friend zone' forever?"

"Yep, that about sums it up," I replied.

"Wow. That sucks," she sighed.

I nodded, "Yes, yes it does, sweetheart."

So, on your worst day at work or, if you're single, out playing the field, keep things in perspective. Take a moment and think, "It could be worse. I could be a Teaser."

The Great Weaning

There comes a time in everyone's life when one needs to leave the comforting bosom of her mother and venture out on her own. On our farm in mid-Ohio, that time comes every October on Weaning Day.

I was out walking my dog, the crisp autumn air and bright blue skies keeping us both moving at a brisk pace, when I noticed a commotion at "The Run-in Barn." The Run-in Barn is a barn where yearling horses, those who have been weaned from their mothers a few months before they turn one-year-old, are kept. The barn opens up onto a field where they can freely run in and out.

On this day, unbeknownst to me, The Weaning was taking place. Our farm manager, Mark, and his right-hand gal, Melinda, were very busy and intense, corralling mother/baby pairs of horses into the barn, paying attention to every move the horses made, lest they be taken by surprise and kicked into next week.

When Weaning Day begins, the poor foals don't know what they're in for. They start the day as usual, grazing with their buddies, nursing and nuzzling with their moms. Quietly, Mark and Melinda take about three or four mares and foals at a time from the field into the barn nearby and then into a large horse trailer. This part is pretty uneventful because wherever the mare goes, the foal—like a clingy toddler—will follow. The trailer then makes the short trip down the hill to The Run-in Barn and, upon arriving, the mare is gently led down a ramp and into the barn, Melinda shushing and patting her all the while. The oblivious babe follows close behind, her nose touching the swishing tale of her mom, per usual.

When they enter the barn, however, the drama begins. The mom is led one way and the babe is led another. Mom starts whinnying and snorting; and the babe wheels around, bewildered by what is happening, looking for mom.

The foal is corralled with other equally-confused youngsters. One by one, about twenty pairs of moms and babes are led through the same process. Soon, The Run-in Barn is filled with panicked, confused foals that are now called "weanlings." It's a bit reminiscent of "the reaping" from *The Hunger Games*, but no one will be forced to fight to the death here.

When I came across this site, it was comical but also pitiful. The weanlings were literally running in circles, bumping into each other, snorting, neighing, and generally trying to figure out what just happened. In the distance, I could hear the retreating sounds of the mares in the horse trailer going back up the hill, whinnying, crying out, as if to say, "It's alright, baby. You're going to be fine. Mommy loves you." Mark turned up the radio (that never actually stops playing) in the barn to muffle the sounds of the neighing moms and to distract the babes so they could settle in.

Inevitably, the babes do settle in and figure it out. The fillies and colts are separated by gender like two single-sex Catholic high schools. In about three days, they are forming new bonds with their peers, figuring out who the leaders are and following them. They pace back and forth like they're at a high school mixer, fillies and colts staring at each other, fillies retreating to a circle to whisper secrets. There's literally a chastity fence down the middle to separate them and make room for the Holy Spirit, I guess.

When I approached the fence of the filly side a few days after The Weaning, the small herd turned in unison to look at me, swishing their tails as if to say, "Oh. My. Gawd. Look. At. Her. Hair."

The alpha horse sauntered over to check me out, and her clique followed. They kind of gave me the up-down until the alpha gal turned dismissively, like she was saying, "What. Ever." It struck me that, in just those few days, they were no longer acting like babies but teens trying to navigate life on their own.

It all felt very familiar and reminded me of so many milestones in my own life where my daughters and I went through the painful process of letting go. I keep thinking back to when I put my oldest daughter—with her freshly scrubbed face and name tag dangling around her neck—on that first kindergarten bus all those years ago. I blew her kisses through the bus window with a lump in my throat, a baby on my hip, and a toddler holding my hand. I think of that first high school drop off, sending her off to the Darwinian playground of adolescence. And, God help me, that gut-wrenching first college drop off when I snot cried all the way home through four states. I thought my heart was breaking then, like a limb had been ripped off my body. I went through each of those phases three times, and it never got easier.

Mark assures me that the mares get along just fine after The Weaning. Like seasoned Irish mothers, they are already pregnant and actually seem to enjoy the downtime before the birthing season starts again in January.

I eventually was fine, too, after weaning my kids. They eventually found their legs and figured it out.

Now, driving them to the airport after holiday breaks, I have a lump in my throat and tears in my eyes. It still hurts to say goodbye. Every time. We kiss and hug goodbye, and I jump in my car, turn up the radio to distract my thoughts, and whisper to them or myself, "It's alright, baby. You're going to be fine. Mommy loves you."

Bobbing and Sobbing

I am bobbing up and down in the deep end of our outdoor pool on a chilly fall day. The hot, hot water of the pool is making steam clouds that hover over the surface, shrouding me in an eerie fog. I am in a fog, indeed. I am sidelined from life with an injury—a herniated disc—and I am in pain, feeling sorry for myself. I inhale the steam slowly, thinking, "Well, at least I get a good facial out of this."

The past several months have been a real ass kicker of worry, sorrow, sadness, and loss in my clan of loved ones. I have been driven by the need to seek out lifelines of joy to offset the rising tide by taking trips as well as nights out with friends, family, and my husband. Trying to make moments count. It's important to keep moving forward.

But then, all of the sudden, the bottom just falls out. Sometimes, you make such a point of seizing the day that the day ends up seizing you. And you find yourself in the deep end of the pool, sobbing.

As I move through the fog, I realize I'm not in charge of anything. Or anyone. "What is the plan?" I reflect, blinking slowly. Then I close my eyes, thinking not just of me, but of the larger picture. Perhaps this is the plan … to be still. To stop moving forward.

I am thinking of a yoga mantra that says, "Be here now in this." I am remembering the biblical phrase that came to me as we kept vigil for my mom for days and days before she died, "Be still and know that I am God."

I bicycle my legs slowly and recall my visit earlier in the week to the indoor pool at the local health club.

I went there for a trial run (to consider joining). There, in the pool, I was suspended by a floaty belt, like a child, choking back tears of back pain as I surveyed my surroundings. The pool was populated mostly by women older than I, committed to taking care of themselves, recovering from their own injuries, attending to each other, building a supportive community—as women do. There was a man in the lap lane, dutifully putting in his time, going back and forth, alone. I thought he was an interesting juxtaposition to the female tribe on my side of the lane markers.

"I am a soggy, pathetic fly on the wall," I said to myself as I treaded water in slow motion, wincing as my back reminded me that all was not well. These women, laughing, cajoling, supporting ... it was clear they had been together for a while. "But I am not one of them," I thought to myself. "I am younger, healthier. I am vital. I am not an injured middle-aged woman. I'm good. I am ... not them. I shouldn't be here." It all made me feel ... vulnerable.

I continued in this vein, listing this way and that—like an untethered buoy in my buoyancy belt, wallowing in self-pity—until I observed a couple of gals chatting in the shallow end. One was in a headscarf, bald as a cue ball, clearly going through chemotherapy. She seemed blasé about it, though I'm sure she wasn't really. She shouldn't have been there, either. She should have been living her life: working, paying bills, cajoling her grandchildren, bowling, whatever.

I peddled past them, and they smiled at me. I was just another gal in the pool.

Back at the farm, in my heated pool with a crystal blue autumn sky overhead, I chuckle at my ridiculousness. I am ashamed of myself as I move my way through the fog.

"Who the hell do I think I am?"

I paddle over to the stairs and slowly, carefully get out of the pool. With humility, I emerge and say to myself out loud, "Get the hell over yourself." I gingerly grab my towel and go inside.

City Dog, Country Dog

Last Halloween, my dog and I were greeting little goblins at the door of our full-time home as they trick-or-treated, and I got a surprising little trick. A gaggle of young girls, bedecked in wings, glitter, and ghostly apparel pushed toward the door, reaching for treats while asking me, "Can we say 'hi' to Taj Mahal?"

Taj is my 80-pound Doberman Pinscher, a visually intimidating specimen. But, as anyone who knows him can tell, he's a complete mush of a dog. He loves people, especially kids.

Not recognizing these little girls as being from my block, I replied, "Oh, sure! How do you know Taj?" I thought they must be new kids at my corner bus stop and visited him as they walked by. But no.

They replied, giggling, rubbing the dog's nose, "Oh, he comes over our house all the time to visit, and we feed him!"

Excuse me? My 80-pound Doberman is, without my knowledge and in spite of our Invisible Fence, roaming our suburban neighborhood freely and has apparently taken up with another family?

"We love Taj!" they exclaimed.

As they drifted away into the darkness, I turned to my guilt-ridden dog. "You …" I hissed at him.

He skulked away silently like Scar from *The Lion King* as if to say, "I don't know what they're talking about, Mom. I've never seen those bitches before in my life."

Taj came into our lives as a precious little 8-week-old pup in the fall of 2012. Shortly thereafter, the farm of our dreams came into our

lives, and ever since, Taj has had to continually switch on and off between the rules
of suburban dog vs. country dog.

In the suburbs, (when he's not stealing away to his other family around the corner) Taj lives a pretty typical life; he chases invading deer out of our backyard, intimidates political canvassers (a huge plus), gets many ear rubs, and generally lays around a lot. Out in the country, however, Taj lives a dog's life to be envied.

As I throw a few things into the car, about to head out to the country, he eagerly jumps into the back seat and assumes a kind of meditative sphinx pose for the hour-and-a-half drive. It's like he's getting into character for his country self. As soon as we arrive on the farm, he's out the door like a shot, peeing on everything he sees. Then he's off to explore the great outdoors like a kid from the '70s. "Come back when the streetlights go on!" I yell after him. Only there are no streetlights out there. He disappears over a hill, galloping like a little rocking horse.

Eventually Taj returns, all sweaty and dirty, smiling from ear to ear and slumps into a contented heap, plumb tuckered out. Who knows what he has seen, chased, peed on or, frankly, eaten? There are wild turkeys, moles, voles, snakes, toads, huge pileated woodpeckers, groundhogs, foxes, and coyotes out there, not to mention the horses that board at our farm. It's a dog's delight. I do know that he makes daily rounds through the barns, tormenting the cats there, scarfing down their cat food like it's manna from heaven. He used to chase the chickens we had, too, until we learned—farm lesson #149—chicken poop is toxic to horses, so they had to go. Before they were evicted, those chickens were an endless source of amusement for Taj. They'd be out minding their own business, pecking in the grass, when along came this exuberant dog, darting through them and sending them squawking, flying in all directions like confetti.

Taj has learned the hard way that the fences penning in the horses are electric. The poor bugger got a rude awakening as a pup when he nosed up to a colt through the fence and got zapped by enough electricity to keep a 1,000-pound animal off the fence. He took off into the woods in a confused panic for about an hour. Maybe that's why he's unphased by a measly Invisible Fence zap … I mean, he's been to the zapping mountaintop. It hasn't dampened his interest in those horses though. I think he thinks they're the biggest darned dogs he's ever seen.

Back in the suburbs, we have rules: no going into the carpeting living room, no sleeping on the couch, no digging the rugs, no wandering the neighborhood. I'm sure it feels like a gulag to poor Taj. And now, with the rules-free farm in our lives, the constant switching of rules and locations has made him a nervous wreck. He's become afraid of some of the floorboards, the icemaker, the broom, the rugs, and his dog bowl, for chrissake. And, I think he's a bit indignant at having to hang out like any other domesticated dog, when he knows he was "born free." Seeing neighborhood dogs with cute little jackets or kerchiefs around their necks, I can almost hear him mutter to them under his breath, "You have no idea what you're missing out there, you silly fools."

For all I know, Taj has a secret farm family, too, that he visits when he disappears over the hills. Are they Amish? Do they call him Eli? Do they feed him farm-fresh eggs and churned butter? There's no way he's doing chores. I can't even get him to retrieve a ball. I'm certain that when they start doling out jobs, he's off like a salty teen. "Y'all, it's been real, but I gotta bounce and get back to the 21st century," he would say to them, galloping away.

Either way, Taj has it pretty good, living his best life in the country and in the 'burbs. Honestly, me too.

A Room of One's Own

During the days of forced togetherness in 2020, I kept thinking of a friend who is obsessed with the "tiny house" movement. These minimalists espouse the belief that we all should eliminate the superfluous stuff in our lives, Marie Kondo-like, and boil ourselves down to our essence in lilliputian tiny houses that are no bigger than 400 square feet. That's barely enough room for a double take, let alone a second thought.

During the height of the 2020 lockdowns when so many of us had our adult children back in our houses, I would chuckle, thinking of my friend and her adult triplets all home at her imagined tiny house and underfoot. I'd think to myself, "I'll bet your normal-size house feels pretty tiny right now, sister!"

I scrolled through tiny house websites back then, captivated by their efficiency. And I looked at photos of young, groovy families who allegedly reside in these tiny houses. I'm all for minimalism, but I don't understand how they can keep this lifestyle up for too many years. What happens when little Tommy becomes a large, lanky teenager and leaves his size 12 sneakers in the tiny living room? Maybe he'll save his allowance for his own tiny house behind the family tiny house.

And when little Rebecca turns into a hormonal teenage terror, would there be enough room for her, her Sephora beauty products, her volleyball gear, AND her attitude? I was picturing the scene from *Alice and Wonderland* where poor Alice's arms and legs are shooting out the windows and doors of the house after she eats those funky mushrooms.

Perhaps tiny houses are really just meant for one person. Now *that* I can understand. I have daydreamed of a space—just big enough for me—where I can write, think great thoughts, and putter about. Uninterrupted. I've been reading Virginia Woolf's iconic *A Room of One's Own* these days. It is revolutionary how this gutsy woman takes on The Man, or rather The Men, logically explaining that, "a woman

must have money and a room of her own if she is to write fiction."
She calmly explains this is due to the fact that women throughout
history and up to that point (1924) were not only often denied a
proper education (and thus the financial independence that gave
them space to create, dream, imagine), but they literally did not have
the room. Nowhere to hide, as it were. They were forever under the
controlling gaze of fathers, husbands, brothers, and children. Or they
were simply too damned busy and exhausted with domestic chores
to create, write, and dream. Exhaustion and misogyny kill a gal's
creativity.

Years ago, when my older sisters were young mothers, they used
to fantasize about pooling their resources and purchasing an
apartment on the lakefront. "The Escape Pod" was to be a retreat
from everyone and everything. They were going to fill it with their
favorite books, movies, and snacks. All the sisters and sisters-in-law
with small children would have keys, but no one else was to know
about The Escape Pod, especially their husbands. By the time I had
young children I totally understood their hideout fantasy. They were
yearning for "a room of their own."

It turns out my husband has had these same urges, and he has a
tiny house of his own: a deer stand. Or, rather, several deer stands.
Each fall, my husband, "Tiny House Tim," has a deer hunting "men's
retreat" at our farm. After the first retreat left him shivering in a
traditional deer stand (which is nothing more than a rickety ski-lift
chair attached to a tree) he discovered these fancy, newfangled deer
stands that are quite literally tiny houses on very long legs. They
have windows with lovely views of the forest (and any incoming
deer), a door, a chair, and some space heaters. Everything a guy
needs to be cozy and all alone in the woods, ready to kill something.
Testosterone meets domesticity. But killing something isn't the only
reason "Tiny House Tim" goes to his bitty abode. He will escape into
these hideaways to just sit and think, dream, listen to nature. When
he returns from his mini retreats, he talks about watching the sunrise,
listening to the forest animals scurry below, and the simple beauty of
isolation.

Back in those nerve-wracking days of the 2020 COVID lockdown, our family of five retreated to the farm property to hunker down. The thought was that with all that space in the house and the acreage around it, we would not only be removed from humanity's coronavirus cooties, but we'd have enough room to navigate around each other. Well, 24/7 time together in a house can make even a large farm feel pretty small after nine weeks. My husband took to "checking on the deer stands" a couple times a week just to get the hell away from all the estrogen in the house. And, because it became obvious that the big, open communal spaces of our farmhouse enabled noise to travel everywhere, our youngest daughter, Rose, started retreating to the tiny house tree stands to FaceTime her boyfriend. I think during those dark lockdown days, it felt nice for her to have "somewhere to go." Like a real date.

Early that fall of 2020, I was out for a hike in the woods and examined a deer stand for myself. I clambered up the ladder, yanked open the door, and hoisted myself up into it. I opened the five little windows to let the breeze move through. And I took out my ear buds, taking a break from incessant chatter. Up there, with a panoramic view of the forest, I sat and listened. Scurrying squirrels, a woodpecker in the distance, the buzz of a fly. A cardinal lilting his distinctive song. A passing butterfly. The constant thrum of pandemic updates went quiet. I looked out into the thick woods and somehow was overcome with emotion. I cried from exhaustion, fear, and gratitude. I couldn't be with my large tribe of people and hug them, touch them, laugh, and cry all over them. I couldn't wave a magic wand to protect them, me, us. But I could be still up there in that tree stand, in that moment, in that tiny house.

I thought of Virginia Woolf writing, "Yet it is in our idleness, in our dreams, that the submerged truth sometimes comes to the top." I thought to myself, "I have to claim one of these tiny houses and create something—a room of my own. I'll also create a book of my farm ramblings." After all, Virginia says, "A lock on the door means the power to think for oneself."

I'm going to need a deadbolt.

Moving On

It was early fall, and I was enjoying one more swim in our farm pool. The air had started to hold the crisp scent of autumn, and as I swam back and forth, I kept my eyes on a bluebird family fervently fussing with their nest. Mrs. Bluebird was feeding a last brood of hatchlings. "Impressive," I thought. "You're heading south soon and here you are squeezing in one more nest of offspring." It got me thinking of how effortlessly birds pack up and move, north to south and back again, year in, year out. "This bluebird family better hurry up," I continued to myself. "Trees are starting to turn color. Time's a-wasting."

I too have a deadline looming on my calendar ... and it's creeping closer. I am in the midst of moving out of my home of 24 years—a house in the middle of an enchanted neighborhood. The home where I raised my family. The home I made my own, little by little, until it had my fingerprints all over every room, metaphorically and literally. It is not a tragic move, not one of necessity or loss, though we are moving into the house of my husband's parents who both passed away over the past two years.

I hate moving. The emotion, the upheaval, the chaos ... I look at my bird friends and wonder, "Do you have stacks of boxes, packing tape, and sharpies in there? Do you have to-do lists on sticky notes? Are you purging before your big move? Or are you just going to, you know, wing it?"

I am having a hard time with the purging because I am a sentimental sot. My writing table faces a painting of my childhood home. Gazing at that painting every morning, I smell my dad's Dial soap aroma, hear my mom's calloused feet shuffling on the kitchen linoleum floors, taste the burnt chicken from our backyard grill, smell the mineral scent of water from the garden hose. I still dream of that house.

The home we are leaving is beautiful, built with love and care by its original owners. It is reportedly a replica of a historic home in Maine. Its triple track windows are inefficient and troublesome. Its basement ceiling is low and weird. And its master bedroom and bathroom are smallish (and have lousy storage). But its woodwork and its bones sing when you walk inside.

As I return home to the task of packing, walking through my home of 24 years ... my beautiful, imperfect home, I notice its lovely details, its solid sense of roots, of permanence. The new owner will change a lot, I'm sure, as I did. I pack, organize boxes, then set things aside for my daughters, for giveaways, for garbage. And I am labeling it all so everything has a place to land on the other side of this chaos.

What will my girls remember from our house? Arguments at dinnertime? Tiptoeing down the stairs on Christmas morning? That wonky brick step outside the mudroom that keeps coming loose?

Change is hard.

Our new home is a home of beauty, calm, comfort, and legacy. I am saying goodbye to the past, but I'm also stepping into a different house full of memories. My husband's parents were in that house for thirty years. Emptying out my in-laws' house, I am struck by the triviality of the stuff we all accumulate through life. They had lovely things—the figurines, the furniture, the candlesticks, etc. But when a life is all over, it's all just stuff, left for someone to go through, pass around, give away.

I am floating from my own memories to my husband's memories, through my in-laws' memories. Looking forward and backward at the same time is giving me emotional whiplash. I keep humming Joni Mitchell to myself, "We go round and round and round in the circle game." I lay down on the floor of the foyer and cry with gratitude, loss, exhaustion, and back pain. I am thankful for the history in the new/old house. I hear my father-in-law's chuckle as I hold his back scratcher, my mother-in-law's nervous humming while I'm emptying out her kitchen drawers.

They say one should move every six years or so just to force oneself to get rid of stuff. I have friends who have moved several times. Some who have moved from city to city so often they are unfazed; they are pros at this. The thought of that much moving pains me. As I am in the midst of that process, I am trying to find the minimalist deep inside of me ... she's here somewhere, under a pile of my old tap shoes and worn, soft t-shirts from the early '90s. I am getting rid of kids' art projects from 20 years ago, books about how to raise children not to be sociopaths, cookbooks never opened but purchased for their culinary porn photos. I grab the cargo pants that I delayed giving away because they may come back in style, and anyways, they do make my butt look good. I make a vow to myself never to purchase anything ever again.

I pack away my mom's spatula with the burn mark on the handle, the china set from our wedding (all fourteen place settings), the teacups from a grandmother I never knew. I think, "What will my own daughters do with our lifetime of stuff? What will be the thing they hold onto from our life together?" It's usually the little inconsequential stuff that holds the most meaning, which is why I lovingly pack my mom's mangled salt shaker that fell down the disposal during the flurry of a post-dinner cleanup sometime in the 1970s ... more than once. It reminds me of the comforting chaos of her kitchen.

I stop at the doorway of my old house, running my hands over the hash marks indicating everyone's growth milestones. Toward the end of this, I'm sure I'll be throwing crap—sentimental and otherwise—into moving boxes. Who the hell knows what I'll unpack from those "Mary's Misc. Stuff" boxes: the pink high top Chuck Taylor sneakers from the bar basketball team I was on in the late '80s or the billowy scarf collection that makes it seem like I am secretly a Stevie Nicks impersonator.

Since our new house wasn't quite ready, we took refuge back at the farm for a few weeks. I checked in on my bluebird family and found they had moved on. I took down their birdhouse and cleaned it out ... nothing was left but twigs and feathery fluff.

I hope they're happy in their new place. I know I will be.

WINTER

Away in a Manger

At this time of year, I can't help but think of Mary and Joseph when I walk through the barns on our farm. I've come to know that stables/mangers are pretty stinky places, albeit warmish. The earthy smells of hay, straw, and fresh poop combine to make quite a pungent bouquet.

I think of Mary, a very young woman with an unplanned pregnancy, waddling around, swollen with child, teetering on the back of a donkey, looking for a room for the night. I think of myself at that stage of pregnancy and remember I could barely sit on the couch, let alone a donkey. I can only imagine the look on Mary's face when they got into Bethlehem so late, and Joseph told her, "Yeah, so … they're out of rooms. But guess what?" I think I would have taken Joe's head off.

"If we had just asked for directions, I'd be in a warm bed right now, pal," she must have said.

I've always had an affinity for my girl, BVM (the Blessed Virgin Mary), my namesake. My mom and dad were big fans, too. My dad carried a copy of "The Memorare," a devotional prayer to Mary, in his wallet. My mom, like any good Catholic mother, had several statues and paintings of the BVM all over her house. Each May, my mom and I would make a May Altar to Mary. I would go outside and pick daffodils, crabapple branches, hyacinth, and tulips. Then I'd deck out what was normally a bar in our dining room, turning it into a beautiful, fragrant altar to Mary. Each day after school I would check on it, cleaning up the fallen petals and sprucing it up.

Perhaps because there were only four TV stations in the '60s, every Christmas Eve growing up, my family would reenact the nativity with a Christmas pageant. Instead of a barn, our nativity scene took place in front of the fireplace in the family room. I debuted as a restless Baby Jesus. But then I went on to own the role of Mary for several years (until grandchildren came along and stole my part). With nine children, it was easy for my parents to populate the cast for their annual pageant: three wise men, Mary and Joseph, two shepherds, two angels. My mom was always the innkeeper, peeping through the shuttered doors with curlers in her hair, shaking her head to mime those infamous words, "No room at the inn." My dad was the cameraman (and miming narrator) with his Super 8 camera and its white-hot lamp beaming down on the action like an interrogator's flashlight.

The shepherds were bedecked with dish rags on their heads (with little mashed potato smears still on them), secured with tube socks or the belt to someone's robe. The angels rocked some white bed sheets—taken right off the bed—with tree garland on their heads for halos. The kings were rakishly handsome in my mother's bathrobes with beards made from dusters turned upside down and tucked under their chins. It was always a surprise to see what the kings' gifts for the babe would be. Sometimes it was a goofy photo, other times it was dinner leftovers. My personal favorite was the time my brother opened a soup pot to reveal not gold, frankincense, or myrrh, but my mother's orthopedic shoes for Baby Jesus. My poor father just kept filming, surely thinking to himself, "And this is why I go to Mass every day. To pray for these slobs."

I was always very serious during the pageant. I dutifully stayed in character as the Blessed Mother, kneeling patiently, sweating in front of the hot fireplace. I doted on my baby doll and tried to ignore my older siblings' sacrilegious behavior. Eventually, it all went to Hell when we gathered for a curtain call in front of the camera, my brothers striking muscle poses, my sisters doing Miss America waves. Then someone would fart, and we'd all collapse into a pileup.

In spite of us all being in varying degrees of devotion to the Church, the Christmas pageant tradition has continued through the nine of us siblings and thirty grandchildren and now, their children.

This year, most of the twenty-seven great-grandchildren will put on the performance, with five babies vying for the coveted role of Baby Jesus. (We may need to have co-Jesuses). The costumes have gotten a bit more sophisticated but not much: old bridesmaids' dresses, lace tablecloths, and some of my mother's fancy lingerie from the '50s are all in the costume box. Talk about sacrilege.

I'm sure my parents are looking down from Heaven with amusement—and hopefully pride—at what they started all those years ago. Somewhere amidst the bed sheets, the tinsel halos, and the farting, something made an impression. The message got through to stop for a moment and think of what happened over 2,000 years ago in a barn in a small town in the Middle East: "Away in a manger, no crib for a bed, the little Lord Jesus lay down His sweet head."

Each December, I walk through our barns, inhale that dank, animal scent, remember BVM, and say, "It all started with you, sister. Thanks. While I'm nowhere near worthy, I'm honored to share your name."

My Camo Life

"Oh, it's happening …" she said smugly. "I knew it would. It starts slowly; you don't even know it. Then, little by little, it takes over your life." My farm neighbor, Judy, chuckled knowingly as she sipped her wine and gazed into the fireplace.

Judy was a city girl some thirty years ago, fell in love with a man from the country, and eventually found herself on a farm, adapting to her new lifestyle. She had forewarned me shortly after we became farm neighbors, and I didn't listen. But she was right. Like a fog, like a thief in the night, camouflage print officially insinuated itself into my house, my wardrobe, my life.

It started as a joke. Shortly after we purchased our farm, we stopped at that mid-Ohio institution, Grandpa's Cheese Barn and Sweeties Jumbo Chocolates, off I-71 in Ashland for some ice cream. On the way there, we passed a sign in front of the outdoor outfitting retailer, Fin Feather and Fur Outfitters, that announced, "They're here! Camo bathing suits are in!"

My daughters and I all sniggered. "Is that a thing?" I said. "Who would want a camo bathing suit? Are they hunting from their pools or something?" I ate my ice cream, secure in the knowledge that I would never buy such a thing.

Over the ensuing five years, however, camouflage began seeping into my life. It began with funny gifts. My daughter bought my husband a camo robe for Christmas. A friend gave him a camo baseball hat with a built-in flashlight in the bill. But then, my husband became "Captain Camo." He bought himself camo hunting gear: a coat, a hat, gloves, a turtleneck. Judy gave him camo Crocs. Pretty soon, my man was disappearing before my very eyes behind a camo compulsion.

I started mocking him by purchasing silly camo things. I thought, "I'll buy the girls matching camo hats and scarves. What a riot!"

But then, I bought myself a camo bathing suit. "It's cute," I said to myself. "And green looks good with my eyes." Then before I knew what was happening, there it was, plain as day, the evidence: a camouflage dog bed, a camo throw on the couch, camo grilling utensils, camouflage slippers, camo sunglasses … It was everywhere at our farmhouse. But the last straw came when I was dashing out the door to go to a yoga class on a cool day, and "Captain Camo" yelled out to me, "Hey, I like your camouflage leggings!"

"These leggings are multi-colored, printed leggings from none other than Athleta, buddy. They're not …" And then I realized, "Oh. My. God. They are. They are camouflage yoga pants."

What compels people to decorate their bodies, their homes, and their pets with camouflage? What are we hiding from?

The only break I see in this camo fever is my husband's growing compulsion to wear flannel, or should I say **a** flannel. For the past four years, my husband has been wearing the same blue-and-black flannel shirt every day. It's been like his security blanket. He only used to wear it on the farm, but he grew so fond of it that he started wearing it everywhere. It got so bad that one of his colleagues at work approached him about it and said, "Dude, what's with the blue flannel shirt?"

So, for Christmas, I decided to buy him more flannel shirts. While I've never been a huge fan of flannel, I have to say, I'm happy with his new wardrobe. It's a comforting reprieve from all that camouflage … and at least I can see him coming now.

Snow Days

This winter was looking like The Winter that Wasn't, until … finally …

"Folks, it's crazy, I know. But it looks like we're getting snow. In January. In Cleveland. Can you believe it? And it's cold. In January. Stay tuned right here for more details," the manic meteorologist said.

I hate to sound officially like an old person, with the "back in my days," but … back in my day, heavy snow and cold weather were expected in winter. In January. In Cleveland. Hell, it was expected from November all the way until June. I recall plenty of Easters spent with a bulky winter coat donned over my frilly Easter dress with my white wicker hat and my open-toed white sandals slipping around in the slush.

I do love a good snow storm… as long as I'm not driving on the highway in one. Lying in bed the other night, I listened for the dull scraping noise of the snow plows going down the street, finally hearing it in the wee early morning hours. It's always barely perceptible, muffled by the thick snowy air. Hearing it reminded me of being a kid, staying up late to watch the news for weather updates (before they were available 24/7), praying for my school to be announced as closed. "Not yet, honey. Better get to bed," my mom would say as I groaned my way up the stairs.

If a snow day was called overnight, there would be an uncharacteristic quiet in the house the next morning. My older brothers would be roused out of bed to hit the driveway and start hauling the white stuff out of the way. It wasn't too much of a burden, though, because there were dozens of other kids doing the same. And soon thereafter, forts and snowballs were being made, strategies of attack planned. And I'd get a snowball to the face from at least one of my brothers. We would finally come in for warmth—cheeks chapped, mittens soggy, bread bags sticking out of our snow boots (that made them easier to slide on, especially with hand-me-down boots that were a little too small). Then it was time to sit down and catch up on the basics: Dinah Shore, Merv Griffin, Phil Donahue.

In later years, snow days became more social affairs. I graduated from the quiet, wimpy swale in our back yard to the titillating teen scene in my friend, Mary Beth's, backyard. The pitch of the sledding hill had to be near 90 degrees, full of a slalom course of trees and a little creek at the bottom of the hill that completely freaked me out. We spent hours careening down that terrifying hill; I can't believe none of us died back there.

There was never a snow like the famous blizzard of 1978. I was 14-years-old. It started as I was walking home from high school. Per usual, I was wearing my uniform skirt with bare legs because no one ever wore tights or—God help me—pants in high school. Half-way through the one-mile walk home, I had to take refuge in a local Methodist church to use their phone and call home. "I can't take one more step. I can't feel my legs. I can't even see to walk. Can someone come get me?" I pleaded. There was eye-rolling and heavy sighing on the other end as my older brother got in the car to come retrieve me.

Back at home, we all hunkered down and watched the storm rage. And rage it did. The snow just kept coming. And the temperatures kept dropping. And dropping. Wind chills were something like 50 below zero or more. One of my older brothers stood, looking out the backyard window up at an enormous elm tree that was being whipped to and fro by the 100-mile-an-hour winds. "That tree is going to come down, Ma," he said as he turned away from the window. No sooner had he entered the kitchen than the tree thundered down, schlumping onto the backyard patio and sending an enormous limb through the ceiling where he had been standing. The patio furniture was instantly dwarfed by the enormity of that tree, making the chairs and table look like dollhouse furniture in comparison—an instant transformation in perspective.

The hurricane force winds found the hole in the ceiling and sent arctic blasts through our home. We all retreated to the far end of the house as that same brother stapled up plastic sheathing to try to keep the winds out.

Several years after that epic blizzard, it was another snowy day when my naughty nephews spent their snow day outside. They snuck over to their next-door neighbor's yard, who was a constantly-complaining pain-in-the-rear with no sense of humor. The boys were inspired to build an anatomically correct snowman and snowwoman. Of course, the snow balls were put in appropriate locations, as were the clumps of grass pulled up from under the snow. In strategic places. My sister (their mom) couldn't stop laughing long enough to reprimand them. I just love that image of those X-Rated snowpeople, staring glassy-eyed out at the quiet suburban street, naked as jaybirds, like snowy pervs.

Now, many, many years later, we had our first snowstorm out at the farm. On that odd weekend, my husband and I were there alone, with no kids or guests. Just the two of us, the dog, the fireplace, and some music. My sister had just been diagnosed with Alzheimer's Disease earlier that week, and I was in mourning. About a year earlier, we had buried my mom, who had suffered from Alzheimer's for over ten years. That same year that Mom died, my mother-in-law was diagnosed with Alzheimer's. As the snow fell hard outside and piled up, I stretched out in front of the raging fireplace, doing yoga, praying, weeping, pleading for a cure, for some answers, for a miracle. "I hate this disease," I yelled at God, at the snowdrifts, at the fireplace, at no one.

The next day, the snow sparkled in the winter sun. Walking out in the crisp, cold air, trudging through the snow, I thought about those snow days of my youth, of my silly nephews, and the heavy weight of my suffering loved ones. "What will we do? What can I do? What will happen?" I ruminated as I trudged on, still weeping. And there it was in front of me ... or rather behind me. "The storms will always come," I thought, looking at my deep footsteps in the newly fallen snow. "It's just like it always has been. Keep going ... one in front of the other. One step at a time."

Journaling on Journaling

One of my favorite things to do on a quiet winter morning out in the country is to get a cup of tea and sit down to write. I have been writing, journaling, keeping a diary on and off for most of my life. I remember writing as an adolescent—with all my angst—about my future, about boyfriends (or lack thereof), about life, etc. I fell off the journal wagon in college. As an English major, I was too busy writing about Shakespeare, Yeats, Dickenson, Shelly, and Fitzgerald. But I picked the habit back up again as an adult and continued spilling my ugly guts and fanciful aspirations down on pages and pages of journals. Sometimes on my own, and later, inspired by books like *The Gifts of Imperfection, Simple Abundance: A Daybook of Comfort and Joy,* and the fantastic *The Artist's Way*. I now start my day every morning by journaling my thoughts.

I was never a scrapbooker, though. I bought the stuff, planned on doing it, wished I could do it, but never got around to being *that mom*. A friend of mine was that mom. She and a couple of her pals would go away once a year for a weekend. They'd bring all their scrapbooking materials and update their childrens' scrapbooks over wine and conversation. I, on the other hand, scribbled just a few things in my kids' baby books: cute anecdotes and things they would say.

My in-laws had a home in Florida and so, for the past thirty years, I've been able to go there, sit on the beach, think, write great thoughts … and a lot of drivel. On a recent trip, I returned to gray Cleveland and discovered, to my horror, that I'd left my journal behind in sunny Florida on my father-in-law's counter. "Oh, good God," I thought. "Please don't let anyone open that notebook up!"

I imagined my father-in-law handing the book over to me, shaking his head and tsk-tsking, "I thought I knew you. But you are a dark, mean, self-absorbed bitch." Or, depending on the page he might open, he might just quip, "Go to the gym already. Stop writing about it. And no, you're not fat."

My father-in-law's helper found the notebook, and I made her swear that she would handle it like toxic waste: dump it in an envelope and send it off to Cleveland.

This brings up the basic conundrum with journaling. If I were to die tomorrow and my children went through my journals as a mother, they would be horrified. Because, unlike my friend who spent hours recording how darling her children were, complete with floral cut-outs and sprinkles on the page, my journals are a record of my frustrations, fears, and anger. Sure, there's also love for my kids, my husband, and our large, rambling families. But if those stinking turds of writings were found and read, years of therapy would surely follow. I'm afraid my kids would all think they've been misled, that deep down, I just hated everyone. Of course, this is not at all the case. It's just that I mind-dump into my journals: good, bad, ugly, saint, sinner ... all of it. Amidst the garbage of complaining, I also scribble on those pages all the best of me: my prayers for my kids, my celebrations of the beauty of life, my many blessings, memories of my parents, my kids, myself. And I'm really working on being more thankful in my journals. Like so many experts advise, it really does lift me up when I do that.

Somehow, I ended up with my mother's sweet, leather-bound diary. It is so very her: starting in a flurry of entries, then tapering off to notes here and there. Hilariously, it looks like she made entries post-facto, because it was signed to her as a gift "from Marie" in 1941, but the entries date from 1939 to 1941. But Marge's entries are revealing of her life at the time. I see her, at 22, just meeting my father ("He sure puzzles me at times.") It is the height of The Great Depression, and she is trying to get a decent job but got beat out by a "college girl." Reading that gave me pause, as I remembered her being very sensitive about not attending college, even though all nine of her children did. "You know, I was in the National Honor Society, and was in charge of tutoring the football players who were struggling," she would often say. I know she always wanted to be a nurse ... and ended up being one in many ways, as the mother of such a large family.

Recently, I nestled down by the fire with my laptop on a cold, snowy day and started to write all about Marge's diary in more detail, wanting to share it with others. I quoted many more entries that were so typically Marge: passionate, bruising easily, loving, funny. I had a page-and-a-half of an essay all written out about it on a Word document. My daughter had borrowed my computer to do something for work. The next day, I went to open my document, and it was nowhere to be found. It was not in the Cloud; it was not in my files. I checked to see if I had written it in a Google document, but no. It was nowhere. My daughter swears she didn't delete it.

Perhaps my mother disapproved of me reading her diary, or at least writing about it for others to know. Perhaps Marge reached through from the other side and slyly pressed the "delete" button on my computer.

I hear you, Marge. I will let further intimacies of your thoughts lay hidden in the pages of your bedraggled, worn little diary. It will be our secret.

Loafing Off

Our farm kitchen is a wide-open space, built to handle crowds, to welcome folks in to cook and eat together. A few years ago, just before St. Patrick's Day, it was covered in flour, butter, raisins, and laughter, for I had invited my three sisters and cousin down to make Irish soda bread together.

For those who are not familiar, Irish soda bread is like a raisin scone in loaf form. It is best enjoyed right out of the oven; smothered with butter and honey; and eaten with a steaming cup of tea. Of course, an old shoe would taste great covered in melted butter and honey, but this smells way better and feels like an Irish nana's hug.

My cousin has the recipe, handed down to her from her mother, who found it in a parish cookbook eons ago. I imagine it was probably originally penned by a square-handed, strong-backed Irish mother with a heart-shaped porcelain face and fair, sparkly eyes.

So, there we all were, soaking our raisins and buttering our pans when my one sister wandered away and decided to crack open our favorite beer, Conway's Irish Ale from my brothers' brewery. After a few sips, she jumped back in to help. The kitchen soon turned into a snow globe as she ripped open bags of flour willy-nilly; darting this way and that; spilling buttermilk across the counter and sending cascades of it onto the floor. We giggled and reprimanded her. "Stop fussing with the flour!" another sister yelled.

"Leave the bloody raisins alone, for the love of God," I said, blinking away the powdery cloud that enveloped us.

She finally drifted away to finish her beer on the couch as we continued to putter about the kitchen, cleaning up after her mishaps as we baked.

It turns out that, unbeknownst to us, my dear sister was in the beginning stages of Alzheimer's. I look back on that day with bittersweet tears. In its ridiculous comedy and tragedy rolled together, it was so very Irish.

The following year, I tried to organize a Soda Bread Sunday, inviting family to bake Irish soda bread together. We were going to donate the loaves to St. Colman Church in Cleveland, my parents' and grandparents' parish—home to baptisms, First Communions, marriages, funerals, prayers of Thanksgiving for my large Irish clan for over one hundred years. When one of my many nieces heard about the event, she gushed, "Of course I'm coming! I wouldn't miss this tradition for anything!" One year in, it was hardly a "tradition," but I loved her enthusiasm.

My esteemed cousin, we'll call her "Mary" (because every Irish Catholic family has at least two of those), owner of "the recipe," taught us the key to baking a successful loaf involves soaking the raisins beforehand, cutting the butter into the flour, and paying attention not to overfill the loaf pans. That last point is important. Just ask my local fire department. They were unanticipated visitors to Soda Bread Sunday when a few loaves were inadvertently overfilled. As they rose, gooey batter spilled over onto the bottom of the oven and quickly burned, sending out billows of smoke when we peeked in to check on their progress. The kitchen full of women scattered into action, screaming, hurriedly opening windows, turning on the exhaust fan, swatting the smoke away from the smoke alarm, shouting obscenities that would make a leprechaun blush ... to no avail. In no time at all, we were visited by a hook and ladder with full-suited, handsome firefighters. "No worries, gentlemen!" my sister shouted out the front door. "It's just Irish cooking!" We tried to pay them for their troubles with fresh soda bread loaves, but after taking in the scene of middle-aged, pasty-faced screaming women covered in flour, they declined.

In mid-March of 2020, just before the whole world turned upside down and then stopped still, my kitchen was full to the brim with sisters, nieces, grand-nieces, a grand-nephew, cousins, a nephew, and a dear friend. At one point, there were about fifteen people in the kitchen, soaking raisins, filling loaf pans, stirring wet mix into dry mix, cracking eggs ... it was chaos. Not "controlled chaos," just straight-up chaos. I was cleaning layers of butter and flour off my counter for days.

We ended up with eighty-five soda bread loaves, wrapped and ready for the St. Colman's Church bake sale. I know legions of cousins across Cleveland who had baked and frozen dozens of loaves in their freezers as well. When the St. Patrick's Day event was canceled due to the shutdown, I gave away some of our loaves to neighbors and friends. But most remained frozen until further notice.

In the days of stillness that followed that shutdown order, that freezer full of soda bread baked with love, laughter, butter, buttermilk, and chaos, was comforting. As my daughters streamed home from the east coast to join in the "hunkering down," that soda bread seemed to hold down the house, like a ballast in a grand Irish ship steaming through the choppy waters ahead.

Moving forward, I am backing away from Soda Bread Sunday. Rather, every March I will bake a few loaves and make a pot of hot tea. I'll cut the loaves; slather the slices in butter and honey; and sit down with friends and family for a good Irish visit. No flying flour, no sticky countertops ... we'll just be together. After all the days of stillness and isolation that followed March 2020, I realize that just being together is an Irish blessing in itself.

Owls and Me

On the eve of New Year's Eve, while driving out of our farm, a grayish black figure flashed in front of our car, forcing my husband to slam on the breaks. "What was that?!" We both screeched. He backed up the car slowly to see what it was.

To our horror, we found it was a beautiful barred owl, splayed out along the drive, his right wing jutting out to the side. My husband, "Bird Man," who knows everything about all birds on the planet for some reason, quickly sprang into action and went into his car for a golf club (after several minutes of swearing).

"What the hell are you doing with that?" I screamed. (I feared he was going to euthanize the owl right in front of me with his 9-iron.)

"Calm down," he barked. "I'm just trying to bend his wing back into shape," which he did, quite adroitly.

We both stood there for about a half hour, me whimpering, cajoling, and whispering to Mr. Owl. "You're okay, buddy. It's going to be fine."

My husband was watching closely, side-eyeing me, probably getting nervous. If this owl died on his watch ... well, it wouldn't be pretty. Even if it wasn't his fault—and it wasn't—he knew I had a thing for owls and got emotional about them.

It all started around the house where we raised our three children; we had frequent owl visits in the arborvitae bushes. We usually couldn't see them, but sitting on our screened-in back porch, we all could hear the owls' distinctive, almost cartoonish hooting in the bushes at night.

My absolute favorite owl call is that of the eastern screech owl, whose call sounds—for all the world—like a whinnying horse. Every time I hear that, I smile at how those owls use audio camouflage, making us think there is a little horse in the bushes.

And then there's the dramatic great horned owl. This fella looks like he is straight out of a movie, like that owl in *Bambi* that was going on about the forest animals being "twitterpated" (translation: horny). I got to see a great horned owl relatively up close when I went on a bird watching excursion years ago with my sisters out to the Magee Marsh nature preserve in Oak Harbor, Ohio. Every May, birders from all over the country converge on this little spot to get cozy with migrating and indigenous birds. One of the geeked-out bird watchers had a small scrum of birders gathering around him, so I squeezed my way into the circle to see what was up. He had a duo of baby great horned owl fledglings in his telescope. They looked so befuddled and unsure of their surroundings that they were beyond amusing. They were actively losing their downy white owlet fluff and were growing mature, brown mottled feathers in splotches. They couldn't seem to figure out if they were supposed to be awake (it was about noon) or asleep, such that their eyes looked like old-fashioned baby doll eyes that would close and open when their head position changed. When I saw their disheveled appearance through the telescope, they reminded me of a couple of college dudes who stumbled home after an all-nighter at the bars.

Yet another owl encounter happened in The Galápagos Islands several years ago. Every night after dinner, my husband and I would grab a glass of wine, pull up an outdoor bench, and sit to watch a short-eared owl swoop and dive—hunting large, bird-sized moths. Every time he grabbed another dinner course, we would break into quiet applause. We were there for a week, and on our walk back to our cottage on our last night there, we came upon the short-eared owl just sitting blithely on the curb of the walkway, as if to say, "Hey, I know you've been watching me all week. Do you have any questions?"

Which brings me back to our farm owl. He sat perfectly still there next to the road that night of our accident for about twenty minutes after impact, his big owl eyes squeezed tightly closed. Then, one eye slowly peeled open as he seemed to strain to focus and figure out what the hell had just happened. "That's it, buddy! You're okay!" I whispered.

As we walked around him, surveying how badly he might be hurt, he peeled open his other eye and then started tracking us in that supernatural 360-degree head turn that owls do. I started to relax. After fanning him with some puffs of air from an old placemat left in the car, he all of the sudden lighted up to the top of our car, gathered himself for a minute, then lifted gently off to the branch of a nearby tree.

My shoulders relaxed as I took a deep breath of gratitude with my hand on my heart. "Bird Man" took a few minutes to watch that owl up in the tree, silhouetted against the winter sky as he wiped his eyes with relief. Then we bid our owl goodnight and happy New Year.

SPRING

To Everything There Is A Season

It is finally, officially spring … and not a moment too soon. I've been living in a season of sadness lately … a season of funerals. Sometimes, it feels kind of biblical, like the story of Job. Just when it feels like it's lifting, another crushing loss comes around.

Years ago, a friend of mine said to me, "I feel like you are always going to baby showers and funerals." She's right. The gifts—and challenges—of being part of a big, rambling family is that there's always a lot of a lot: births, baptisms, First Communions, illnesses, hospitalizations, weddings, funerals, burials. Like shark teeth, it all just keeps coming and coming. In the space of the 18 months from 2019 to 2021, we buried four family members and a childhood friend.

Living through these funerals, and retreating to our farm for a rest at the end of it all, I am reminded that a farm is all about the cycle of birth, death, and rebirth. Our farm, especially. It is a horse breeding farm, so starting each January and continuing on until May, a barrage of babies is born. And yet, in all that joy and hope, every now and then there is tragedy. Despite vigilant husbandry, sometimes a mare will die in childbirth. Or a foal. And once in a great while, both mare and foal will not make it. It's always a somber time on the farm when that happens. Much like when a family member passes, it is exhausting, depleting. But no funeral arrangements for them. Life goes on. There are more baby horses to take care of.

As I pour more hot water into my mug of tea, I see that the stark trees which were barren, silhouetted against the silent sky all winter, are now leafing out. There is a new, soft green and pink hue to the woods. Springtime is the season of rebirth.

I scroll through my photos on my phone, taken from all of the funerals. I stop on a photo of a sweet, toothless, wet-mouthed baby— my niece's daughter—smiling ear to ear, blissfully unaware of all the sadness around her.

Just like the green/pink woods and the latest baby foals in the barns. New life. Hope. It will be okay.

Wildflowers and Butterflies

For the past several years, I have been pining for a wildflower garden on our farm. Our farm manager, Mark and his father are passionate about orderliness, so they have resisted. They love the clean, organized lines of a freshly mowed lawn. Acres and acres of green, tidy pastures adorn our farm and I, too, love it. It is soothing, predictable, orderly.

But I have been yearning for an unrestrained, wild, colorful field of wildflowers out there ... and this past spring, I got my wish. I finally convinced my husband that, of our expansive acreage, we could spare a small patch to indulge my floral fantasy. We walked around the property, trying to find the right location that was out of the way of farm duties like feeding horses, hauling hay, and spreading manure, but in the line of sight from the house. We found a perfect spot, just beyond our vegetable garden, down a slight swale.

The next day, our farm neighbor, Eric (a real farmer, not poser farmers like us) volunteered his services. He dredged a patch of grass, turning over the rich soil beneath it. He then tamped it down and scattered the seed evenly over the roughly 20' x 60' area. "Now we wait," he said. It was all up to Mother Nature to water and feed the field with sunlight.

By mid-summer, the field indeed came to life. And it was glorious: red, blue, purple, orange, and pink flowers were in a cascading cycle of bloom. The juxtaposition of my wildflower meadow's wanton disorder against the tidy green acreage around it made a stunning piece of art—framed in a green mat. Every time we went to the farm this past summer, I immediately visited my wildflower field to cut flowers. Sure, there were weeds in there, but honestly, aren't wildflowers really weeds with better PR? Unlike my more manicured garden at home, I left the weeds alone in this garden. Songbirds, hummingbirds, bees, praying mantises, and more began visiting.

My favorite interlopers are the butterflies. These silent, beautiful beings are like quiet angels passing through. Seeing a butterfly in nature is akin to seeing a rainbow; it induces delight and awe in everyone. One of the reasons I wanted that wildflower garden so badly was because I knew monarch populations were dwindling due to loss of habitat. The monarch butterfly has an extraordinary migration from North America to Mexico every year that is a logistical marvel. No individual butterfly completes the entire round trip. It is more like an insect relay race, with female monarchs laying eggs for a subsequent generation to complete the migration. Four generations are involved in the annual cycle.

When my kids were little, we had a special interaction with a butterfly. Each winter, we would make a yearly pilgrimage to Butterfly World in south Florida while we were there visiting my in-laws. Butterfly World is essentially a zoo for butterflies, with enclosed atria housing species from all over the planet in simulated natural habitats. One year, we bought a butterfly chrysalis to bring home and watch the miracle of rebirth that happens as the insect sheds its old way of life and emerges resplendent, transformed, victorious. About a week after bringing the chrysalis home, my toddler daughters and I sat transfixed for hours—or at least I did—as the insect started the slow, miraculous process of emerging from its hibernation. The girls ran in circles, squealing, driven crazy with anticipation and frustration, while I kept them from trampling the fragile little guy. When the butterfly finally completed its transformation, it sat for a while, all wet and gooey, drying its wings in the sun.

And then...it was off...

Over the last few weeks this fall, my beautiful wildflower meadow has had a final burst of colorful energy. With the end of the season nearing, it's been like a grand finale of explosive color. Cosmos, New England Aster, Milkweed, Coreopsis, and Cornflower have been giving it their all before settling down for a long winter slumber. Like the autumn colors, I find their impending hibernation to be bittersweet.

In the midst of this wretched pandemic time, I find myself, like my daughters with the butterfly, running in circles from the frustration and angst of just wanting to get on with it already. I'm having trouble writing, thinking creatively, and being patient. Perhaps I should stop trying to make orderly, well-manicured sense of this time and just let it all go. Maybe it's best to take a cue from that butterfly and that wildflower field and pull in; cocoon myself emotionally and creatively; let the field of my mind lie fallow; and metaphorically fall back into the earth.

Perhaps this time of isolation, contraction, and withdrawal will reveal something beautiful on the other side.

At the very least, there will be a wildflower garden to look forward to next spring.

News Flash: I'm Irish

"Oh, wow. It looks just like Ireland," many visitors say.

Well, kind of … just drop some stone walls and a lot of wooly sheep in there and yes, our farm does look a lot like the rolling, green hills of Ireland, especially as we are on the verge of spring. This feels appropriate because—news flash—we're kind of Irish.

My husband and I gave our family the gift of "23 & Me" genetic testing kits. The results are in: we're really, really Irish. Grace is 91.6%; Ginny is 90.8%; Rose is 96.8%. My husband is a mere 85%. I am the proud Irish Queen at 98.1%.

I'm actually a little surprised my results aren't 100%+ Irish. I mean, I've always known my people were Irish. Like so many in Greater Cleveland, both my parents were children of Irish immigrants from County Mayo. So immersed in my Irish-ness was I as a youth that, when filling out biographical information on standardized tests in grade school, I was confused, looking over the options: Caucasian, Black, Asian, Native American. I raised my hand and asked the teacher, "Um, I'm none of these things. I'm Irish."

"You're Caucasian, honey. You're white," she said.

"Hmm. Go figure," I muttered to myself, baffled, though I was sure she was mistaken.

I took my Irish-ness for granted when I was young; I had this internal vision of myself as a different ethnicity… Polynesian or Puerto Rican. I adored the musical *West Side Story* and thought of myself as that famous Shark girl, Anita, or at the very least Maria. But when I was in that play in college, they quickly cast me as a Jet girl.

Growing up, I thought everyone used words like "amadán" (moron);

"nabicantch" (I have no idea how to spell this, but it means, "quiet now, someone's coming"); "pogue mahone" (kiss my ass); and "eejit" (idiot). There was also a particularly lyrical word for a woman's nether regions that my maternal grandmother reportedly used, which I will refrain from using here, just in case it offends. I seriously didn't even know any of those phrases were Irish until I read them in the novel *Trinity* (by that great Irishman, Leon Uris, who is Jewish) in my late 20s. When it was published in 1975, *Trinity* was all-but-required reading for Irish Americans.

When I moved into adulthood, I was not especially looking for an Irish American lad. I considered myself a citizen of the world, after all. (I speak Spanish, I love to travel, and I enjoy meeting people and learning about different cultures.) But then I met this guy with the map of Ireland all over his face and what my father referred to as "poet's eyes," and I fell.

My husband and his clan identify as Irish American, but I have to say, I've always been a little snobby about that. I mean, they've got German roots, English roots, Texas roots—whatever that means. (My brother-in-law tells everyone he's half Irish, half Texan.) But when my husband got his genetic results back, I was impressed; 85% Irish is pretty respectable.

To be clear, my family was never one of those families with what I call TIP, "tacky Irish paraphernalia," all over the house. Sure, we took off school every year to go to the St. Patrick's Day parade downtown, sit at my aunt's kitchen table, and share family stories all day. That tradition morphed into a larger gathering where my clan drinks beer together at a large Irish St. Patrick's Day hooley. Yep, I use the word "clan" a lot. And "hooley." Yes, I gather a group in my kitchen every year to make dozens of loaves of Irish soda bread.

And okay, my own kids took step dancing classes. Then there's all that Irish stuff ... Belleek china, some Waterford crystal, some crosses of St. Brigid, the obligatory Irish knit sweaters, a couple Chieftains CDs.

Yes, as I write, I have a big fat green shamrock on my front door. Oh, and two of my brothers own a brewery.

Okay. We're pretty over-the-top Irish.

When we acquired our farm property and built a new barn for the horses there, my husband insisted that we put shamrocks on it. I thought it was kind of hokey, but I have to admit, I do like it now. And it turns out that our farm manager Mark's wife is a beautiful blonde-haired, blue-eyed Irish lass herself; her father was born in Ireland. So the shamrocks fit in well.

All this got me thinking. Our farm is a horse-breeding farm. Genetics play a very important role there. Mark and his staff pay a lot of attention to bloodlines. So, at least on our farm, at 98.1% Irish, I guess I'm darned near a thoroughbred.

Cardinals and Angels

I am hearing the cardinals sing again, from the tippity tops of the barren trees. Cardinals always remind me of my parents, especially when I see cardinals in early spring because that's when each of my folks went to heaven, 13 years apart. My dad loved nature, and after he died, it seemed we were always seeing cardinals at just the right times. It's as if his angel was a cardinal and would make surprise visits to give us encouragement or just to say "hello" (though I'm not sure Big Jack would ascribe to this pantheistic viewpoint). Once, when we were having a heavy family meeting after my dad died; my mom, siblings, and I were at the homestead, huddled in Mom's back room, deep in weepy, emotional discussion. All of the sudden, there was a pecking at the window on the large, sliding glass doors looking out to the backyard. We stopped talking and looked up to see a fat, red cardinal, hovering in the air like a hummingbird, frantically tapping at the window. "Let me in! I have something important to say!" It was the darndest thing.

But none of the bird/angel visits were more dramatic than when my mother was in the long, painful process of dying. It was one of those cold, blustery days of very early spring in the Midwest. Our favorite priest stopped in to give Mom her last rights. The group of us huddled around her, tearfully getting ready to say goodbye, praying "The Hail Mary" and Psalm 23: "Even though I walk through the valley of the shadow of death, I fear no evil, for You are with me; Your rod and Your staff, they comfort me." The psalm doesn't mention a cardinal, but in this case, it should have.

Mom's bed was directly in front of a window on the second floor of the facility where she was staying. Suddenly, I noticed something out of the corner of my eye and instinctively looked out the window. There, just above Mom's head, was a bright red cardinal on a tree branch, looking right into the window. A calm came over the dimly lit room. I felt the presence of God and of my dad, beckoning my poor, suffering mother, "It's okay, Marge; let's go." Just as I was focusing on that beautiful, bright red male cardinal, in swooped a female cardinal, who lighted right next to him on the branch. I signaled to my siblings what was happening right outside the window, and we all continued praying, holding hands and laugh-crying at our little avian miracle. The cardinal couple stayed there until we were finished with our prayer and then silently flew away. Our priest friend was amused but didn't seem too surprised. He was an old man himself and I got the impression he'd been witness to all sorts of quirky visitations and miracles.

Since Mom left to join Dad, I now see both male and female cardinals at opportune times: when I'm in despair or troubled especially. I had a health scare a few years back and was praying in the car as I drove. Then there they were; cardinals swooped down in front of my car, just letting me know Mom and Dad were near. God heard me, all will be well.

I've discovered that I am not alone, that the cardinal is widely known as a sign from loved ones who have passed on, a symbol of God's love, an angel visiting. The backyard of our home is often filled with cardinals, nesting in our arborvitae, singing one of their distinctive, piercing melodies from the treetops. That song is so optimistic, so beautiful and self-assured. And it is said that cardinals mate for life, which makes their sightings all the sweeter.

The Birthing Season

The farm staff pace back and forth. They take turns sleeping restlessly in a cushy recliner, one eye open, watching the pregnant mothers, waiting for something to happen. The mothers groan and ache; their bellies are swollen, overfull. Days come and go with nothing happening but watching, waiting.

Springtime is the birthing season on our farm, and the barns are pretty much maternity wards for horses. Pregnant mares populate each stall. Emotions are high: expectation, nervousness, relief. It's an exciting, beautiful time … but it's a lot of work for our farm manager, Mark, and his staff. Starting in January, the babies come, one by one, slowly at first. Then, the pace picks up. And by March and April, they're coming so fast, Mark's team can barely keep up: one, two, sometimes five foals a week. They nearly always come in the still of night, just to make it more challenging.

I was walking through the barn the other day, past about six stalls with overripe pregnant mares, each impatiently waiting for nature to take its course. They paced back and forth, aching under the weight of their load. I stopped to chat with one gal who was past due. We could tell she could go any minute; her teets had already started dripping milk, but still, nothing was happening. "Oh, I've been there, honey. I know …" I whispered to her. She shuffled up to me, putting her nose against the iron grate that separated us. I bent my head toward her; she did the same, and we both stood there, foreheads touching, our breath sending little clouds into the icy night air. "You're almost done, sweetheart. Hang in there," I told her.

Standing there with that mare, my mind went back 20-something years. I remembered that feeling well. I knew that the mare's pelvis was feeling like an egg, slowly cracking open. I knew her ankles were swollen, her legs buckling, her mind a little crazed. Perhaps, like me, she was craving gallons of ice-cold orange juice? This mare was a veteran, though, so she knew what she was in for … but that didn't take away the discomfort, the anxiousness.

My husband and I have been blessed to have witnessed several births on the farm over the past few years. When we get the call that one of the mares is giving birth, we jump in the four-wheeler to race a mile down the gravel road, skidding to a stop at the barn and hopping out. Many times, we just miss the actual birth. (I wish my own labor and deliveries had gone so quickly.)

But every so often, we'll get there just in time to see the magic. The mare is lying down; her water is already broken, and a little pair of hooves is jutting out of her. Mark will rub her belly to encourage and calm her. Then he will grab the baby's hooves and gently coax him out.

If all goes well, and it usually does, the foal is born quickly, sliding out all slippery and confused, and the mare is soon licking it clean. The newborn foal is about as big as our Doberman, though with legs almost as long as its mother's, but spindly—nowhere near as beefy and strong. The babe will lay there for about a half hour, wet and shivering, getting used to breathing air, enjoying the tongue bath from its mom. Soon, the baby is testing out his legs. It's like that scene in the movie *Bambi* when he's wibbly-wobbling all over the ice. The newborn is unsure, struggling, falling, getting back up again. But, in about an hour and a half, that little baby is up, nursing for the first time. It's amazing, beautiful. It never gets old.

The mares on our farm are broodmares, so they go through this process many, many times in their lives. My hat is off to them; I only gave birth three times. Compared to my sainted mother, who gave birth nine times, I am a complete minor leaguer—an amateur—and Mom wasn't shy about reminding me of that. "All single births for me, no twins," she often would say, implying that with twins, you got two babies for the labor of one, like it was cheating or something.

I remember when I was pregnant, giving birth and nursing … I felt a connection to all mammals on the planet, from dogs to elephants to horses. Oftentimes, I felt like a bosomy cow. "We are all the same," I thought. "We conceive, gestate, give birth, and nurse our young."

My oldest sister says that pregnancy and childbirth is the "great equalizer." No matter your zip code, race, or creed, we women all go through the same thing. From cavewomen thousands of years ago to movie stars today.

Two of my three babies came in the early spring. And both of my parents passed in the early spring. While Ohio springs are not easy—I remember plenty of snowy Easters growing up—springtime is a poetic reminder of the cycle of life: death, birth, renewal, hope. And yet, hope is just part of early spring. Each year, just when we cannot take one more day of slushy, snowy, gray days, ferns yawn out from the ground, as if stretching their arms after a long winter's nap. Trees explode in slow motion, opening up their leaves in celebration of the longer days. And the earth miraculously, inevitably reawakens and is born again.

Wild Turkeys

Wild turkeys used to be an interesting novelty. When our daughters were little, they were out hiking with their dad and came across a flock of wild turkeys. "Girls, look! Those are wild turkeys," my husband whispered to them.

Our youngest was about three-years-old and was fascinated by these strange, dark, prehistoric-looking creatures. On the car ride home later, she took a swig from her sippy cup and whispered, "Dad … those turkeys were wild!" as if to say they were crazy, off the hook, unhinged partiers.

In the years since, I've been noticing turkeys all over the suburbs: walking past strip malls, hanging out in backyards, outside the doctor's office. Much like suburban deer, wild turkeys are very incongruous in civilization and frankly, they're a bit surly. Out in the country, they nibble their way across cornfields and woodlands. They stick close to the ground. They have wings but don't use them much. They do jump, rather than fly, up into trees to roost at night and over fences when need be; but mostly, they just grouse around, hunting and pecking for food.

Once we purchased our farm, my husband was super excited to hunt wild turkey in the spring. He'd never been turkey hunting, and our farm neighbor, Eric, was stoked to show him the ropes. Besides the new challenge of shooting a wild turkey, my husband would get to wear as much camo as he wanted. It seems that, unlike deer, who are a bit dim and don't really take notice of hunters in their bright orange gear, wild turkeys are pretty wily, have great eyesight, and are hard to fool. So, turkey hunters get all dressed up like Viet Cong and stalk down the enemy: Tom Turkey.

While I've never cooked a wild turkey, I'll never forget my first experience at roasting a regular turkey. I was a young mother, about to host roughly 50 family members. The fact that I'd never roasted a turkey didn't dissuade me. I thought, "How hard could it be … right?"

That day, I was up early. I had already set the tables and was ready to tackle the bird. I washed him in the kitchen sink like a chubby, slippery newborn baby, and then I dried him thoroughly. My sister-in-law down the street was doing the same thing for her family, and we kept calling each other for reassurance on what the hell we were doing.

"Okay, I've washed him and dried him. Now … where are the damned giblets?" I asked her.

"I don't know. I've been looking for them too," she said.

"Wait … I think I found them," I cried. "They're in the cavity. Just reach in and grab them."

"Eww … Okay, got 'em," she said with victory in her voice.

"Wait … I thought there were more. This is just his neck," I said, confused. "I guess maybe they just throw that other stuff away."

We each proceeded merrily along, basting, rubbing, stuffing, and roasting our respective birds. About two hours into the process, there was a commotion in my mudroom hallway.

"Stop!" someone screamed. I turned around to see my sister-in-law and her sister, falling down, laughing hysterically. "We found them!"

I turned around. "What the …?"

"The giblets! They're in the butt!" they screamed in unison.

I gingerly opened the oven and pulled the turkey out to check. Sure enough, there they were, giblets steaming in a paper bag shoved up his arse. I quickly extracted them, threw them in with the neck parts I had simmering on the stove, and then returned my turkey to the oven.

"Good Lord," I thought. "How humiliating for Mr. Turkey." This was a bird that Benjamin Franklin lobbied to make our national bird, impressed by the turkey's intelligence and stature. (Take that, Bald Eagle). Now, the poor species have been domesticated and humiliated with kibbles and bits shoved up their downsides. Quite a fall from grace, I would say.

But he was tasty.

Breast of Times

I feel a certain affinity with the nursing mares in the barns and fields of our farm for they, like me, are mammals.

When I had my first child, I remember thinking "I am a mammal! I nurse my young!" It's incredible to think about. Watching a newborn foal struggle to its feet and instinctively find its way to nurse its mother is to believe in nature, survival, resiliency.

When I was a new mother, I didn't know exactly what I was doing. Fumbling my newborn baby to my breast, I was scared, excited, curious. But my baby girl knew exactly what to do. Just out of the womb, she looked me straight in the eye and immediately started rooting around for that breast. More than a week overdue, the in-utero buffet was no longer cutting it. She. Was. Starving. She quickly found what she was looking for and started going to town. "Oh, my!" I thought. "So this is how this goes!"

A few days later, I remember waking early one morning to a completely transformed bustline. This sudden, immediate switch from normal, pregnant boobs to—BAM!—porno boobs was dramatic. And painful. Weepy, sleep-deprived, and desperate, I pleaded with my husband to go to the drug store to pick up a breast pump I had reserved to rent. Eager to have something useful "to do," off he went.

I shuffled around for the next few hours, gingerly putting ice packs and cabbage leaves onto my swelling chest. My baby was getting increasingly frustrated. My breasts were so enormous and hard that it was torturous for us both. It must have felt like she was nuzzling a hot, huge boulder. I felt like a Macy's Day parade float, ready to levitate under my titanic tatas. "Where in the blazes is he with that bloody breast pump?" I cried.

Just when I thought he had skipped town, in walked my husband, "Father of the Year."

"Babe! I'm home!" he yelled triumphantly. He strode into the TV room, where the baby and I both were whimpering in frustration, carrying a very large box. "I figured we were going to be spending more time at home now, so .... ta-da!" He unpacked a large television on the table in front of me. "I got us a new TV!" he exclaimed, as if he'd just gone out and felled a bison for dinner.

"Where the hell is my breast pump?!" I screamed.

He looked away. "Oh ... I forgot about that."

It's a miracle I didn't kill him. But I needed him to go get that breast pump, so I restrained myself. The rest of that afternoon was a biblical scene of crying, gnashing of teeth, and blaspheming.

The breast pump came by the end of that day ... without bloodshed, I am proud to say.

Once I got over the learning curve of bleeding nipples, feeding schedules, and wardrobe choices that included shirts with trap doors, I found that breastfeeding was a natural, beautiful thing to do. Watching mares and foals have impromptu feedings, whenever and wherever they needed to, I found myself envying the ease and lack of weird sexualization that we human female mammals have to endure when feeding our young as nature intended. These gals were pros. They got the job done efficiently, while grazing, taking in the sun, occasionally snapping their heads back to reprimand a youngin' getting too aggressive.

When my beautiful first child was about two months old, we went on a trip to Wrightsville Beach, North Carolina. My husband was thrilled to be back in his college town with his new little family, and

I was thrilled to be out of the house. There we sat at a local seafood restaurant, barely anyone there, when our baby started getting fussy and hungry. I grabbed a young waitress, asking, "Hey, can I just sit in that room over there and breastfeed my baby?" I assumed she was on my side, ready to help out another woman.

"Well, you can just use the bathroom," she sniffed, then walked away.

The next scene was one of me sobbing in a bathroom stall, my beautiful infant screaming in frustration because, being so upset myself, I couldn't relax enough to nurse her. "Why in hell did I ask permission to feed my own child?" I muttered to myself. Rookie mistake.

What in blazes is wrong with people? Why can't a human mother feed her baby naturally, just as those mares and foals on the hillside, wherever and whenever she wants or needs to? We are both mammals. Mammals create milk to feed to their young. I am not "Breastfeeding Mother of the Year" by any means. I have dear friends who lapped me in the Breastfeeding Olympics, feeding their kids well into toddlerhood. For me, when a kid puts down their bologna sandwich and whines, "Mom, gimme some boob," it's time to pull the plug.

This new generation of young mothers are impressive in their use of technology. They are experts at bringing their pumps to work, disgorging before they go out for the night, and pumping discreetly in the corner of family gatherings. Breast pumps now are double-barreled, efficient marvels that young mothers can purchase, not send their doddering husbands out for rentals. Also, these moms have the benefit of Netflix for those late-night feedings.

Which makes me think: I guess maybe my husband was right ... you do end up watching a lot more TV.

SUMMER

Papa Was a Garden Gnome

We have a garden at our farm. Not like my suburban garden—full of hosta, spiderwort, and hydrangea—but a "garden garden," a vegetable garden. The previous owners were real farmers and had a huge, lovely vegetable garden, overflowing with tomatoes, squash, beans, and a beautiful strawberry patch. While I'm a halfway decent suburban gardener, I'm a lousy farm gardener because you have to tend a farm garden. Daily. The first year we tried, we ended up with a bunch of weeds that had a few spindly vegetables fighting for existence.

Whenever I work in the garden, I think of my dad. Jack, a son of Irish immigrants, had a deep love for the land—nurturing it, fiddling around with the soil and whatnot. It's not like he was a farmer by any means. Perhaps it was his Irish ancestral longing to have land of his own, as his own parents and forefathers were denied that right back in the old country. His own father, whom I never knew, owned a "farm" outside Cleveland that was nothing more than a patch of land, somewhere to go to get away from industrial era Cleveland for fresh air and picnics. Jack grew up to be a lawyer, an estate planner, a numbers guy. But he loved a beautiful yard, a large expanse of freshly cut grass with beautiful flowers tucked in around it.

When I was two-years-old, he moved our family of eleven into a house on an acre of land in Rocky River, Ohio, which was a good-sized plot for a suburb. Our family spent the next 33 years working every square inch of that yard: weeding it, cutting it, planting it, trimming it. With nine kids and an ever-growing army of grandchildren providing free labor, Jack would dream up all sorts of projects to direct us. He had five sons who were coming of age at the height of the mid-'60s. Any parent knows that a busy teen is a tired teen and a tired teen is much less likely to be a naughty teen. (My brothers proved that axiom wrong, but still, it was a good thought.)

So, it was Jack's mission to keep us all tired.

Every Saturday growing up, our yard was abuzz with activity. My older brothers were in charge of heavier manual labor—cutting the grass (a never-ending chore), hauling grass clippings. My job was to weed the front myrtle patch. And the grass. And the flower beds. It was a Sisyphean chore that was never, ever done. We all were sure Jack sprinkled weed seeds around that garden at night just to keep us all busy weeding the damned thing all summer long.

I was the only person I knew whose job it was to weed the "wild grass" from the front lawn. On scorching summer days, as friends would pedal by our house on their way to the pool or to Dairy Queen, I would be bent over, like a crop worker picking cotton, a hot sunburn cooking the base of my back where my t-shirt would ride up. Hard work for a gal who was up until 1 a.m. watching Johnny Carson with her mom. (There are benefits to being the youngest of nine.) Any friend who wanted to play got roped into weeding with me, so as to free me from my chores sooner. By the end of the summer, they too had the "mark of Jack," that same lower back sunburn.

Nothing pleased Jack more than a yard full of child laborers whom he rewarded every Saturday with freshly grilled "skin-on wieners." To this day, I have no idea what those were, but of course it always sounded dirty. They were delicious, but after being bent over in a hot, humid yard all day, sunburnt, freckled, and dehydrated, I would have eaten a boot.

One of my other jobs in the yard was planting little pockets of flower gardens around. Because I was the youngest and smallest, Jack thought it was cute that I could fit under the bushes, squeeze behind the grill, duck in just under a window. I would battle the midges and mosquitoes and then, like an urchin chimney sweep, I'd emerge all dirt covered and sweaty, but the task was done—a tiny begonia bonanza under the mushroom lights over on the swale. "Looks great, Mary," he would say from the comfort of his chaise lounge, sipping hot tea on a muggy summer day. I have to admit, it did look pretty as I headed in to hide from Jack, put an ice pack on my head, and apply

Noxzema to my sunburn in the air-conditioned living room.

God, I hated working in that yard. But of course, I'm thankful for
it now. I am thankful for the time together with my family, all of
us pissing and moaning and cursing under our breath. Talk about
bonding. I am thankful for the lesson of hard work, working together
for a shared goal. I am thankful for the lessons of cherishing the land,
walking gently upon the earth—reducing, reusing, recycling. (A man
who was years ahead of his time, Jack had three large compost piles
at the back of the property to recycle grass clippings, leaves, and yard
waste.)

And above all, I am thankful for a dad who was wise enough to know
that all the manual labor wasn't about the yard at all. It was about us.
About keeping a large family busy, engaged, in touch, humble. And
yes, tired.

Nowadays, with the help of real farmers who know what they're
doing, we've figured out the vegetable garden (raised beds and dark
fabric covering!). As I plant my little plots, weed my garden and look
out over the awesome beauty of the sun rising over the mist-covered
hills of our farm, I think of Jack, smiling down on me, his arms
akimbo with that big Irish grin.

Momma's Got a Gun

I shot a gun today. I didn't want to, but for some reason, ever since we acquired this farm, my middle daughter, Virginia, has been all about learning how to handle and shoot a gun. My husband, "Quick Draw McGraw," the father of three girls and outnumbered by women in the house for 28 years now, wiped the stunned tears from his eyes. "Sure, princess. We'll shoot a gun."

So, there we all were at our farm neighbor's shooting range. I had never even touched a gun, never wanted to. Our neighbor patiently explained the safety measures of a gun. Firstly, one's own mind. Secondly, one's own finger.

That was precisely what scared me about guns (and me with a gun more specifically). My mind can wander toward to-do lists, grocery lists, house projects, and such any time. That's just the kind of stuff that could end up with me shooting off my foot.

At any rate, there I was watching my beautiful, lanky daughter—a healthcare professional—don the protective eye gear and ear covers as she held a revolver in her hand. Then a pistol. Then a Glock, for the love of God. It was nauseating to see at first. But she did a fine job, and was impressive. She didn't shoot me, herself, or anyone else.

Then daughter number one joined the party. Grace, a young, vocal Liberal, an artist, was dressed in shorts and a yoga shirt on her petite frame. Having her handle a gun was like seeing a talking dog or something. She took to it like a natural, though, with deadly aim, which made me nervous for the next dinnertime political debate.

Next it was my turn, and by now, I was intrigued. If lanky Virginia and yoga master Grace could do it, so could I. (Rose was sitting this one out, watching suspiciously from the four-wheeler.) When I was handed the gun, it felt heavier than I thought but also familiar.

"Oh! It feels like those water pistols at the shooting gallery at Cedar Point Amusement Park!" I muttered. Except it wasn't.

I refused to let my mind wander and became very serious. I looked at the target.

"Does it have to be a human form?" I thought, looking at the paper target in the distance.

Rest the butt of the gun in the crook of your shoulder and grab the handle. Use your other hand to grab the handle as well, and then point your finger along the shaft. Turn off the safety. (Wait. Argh!) That's when it became scary. Aim down the barrel at your target and, just like it's a water pistol, pull the trigger.

Yep. I shot a gun. Several times. Lots of times. And I am a good shot as it turns out. Go figure. Take that Annie Oakley! (We're both from Ohio.) When the nausea settled down, the adrenaline kicked in. I took a look at the target and found I shot that mother right down the middle. Who am I? Scarface in yoga pants?

I have to say, I understand why people find this … what is it? Entertaining? Exhilarating? Liberating? While I found it actually okay to shoot at a piece of paper and empty beer cans, I have no desire to kill anything.

Our farm is in "gun country." Those of us who are ignorant of guns and didn't grow up with them or have any interest in them can make certain assumptions about folks who do. And guess what? They're not hill jacks, simple, or dangerous … or at least not any more than non-gun people can be. In chatting with farm neighbors, I have found that when one lives out in the country and is some 45 minutes or more away from the police, one is inclined to be prepared to take matters into one's own hands. And many people out in the country hunt, so they practice shooting on the weekends. (Yep, hearing the pop! pop!

of gunfire in the distance on a beautiful Saturday morning takes getting used to. Just ask my dog.) In fact, it seems most folks out here "carry."

When my husband, "Quick Draw McGraw", was with a group of friends from home, introducing them to some local farmers, a "city slicker" friend mentioned aloud, "I've never shot a gun. Never even touched one."

Immediately, without hesitation, about a dozen men put their guns on the table. "It's different out here," one declared.

Our farm manager, Mark (aka "The Sheriff") is always packing because we have lots of horses on the property and (farm lesson #104) raccoon and skunk poop is highly toxic to horses, so those suckers are going down on sight before they poison the horses. It took me a long time to realize that when our manager says, "Old Rocky Raccoon died of lead poisoning," he means that he shot that little varmint. Shot him dead. Don't mess with that man. Truth be told, out here alone at night, it is comforting to know that he is packing. It just is.

Since that day, my husband keeps urging me to get my CCW permit (carrying a concealed weapon), if only to get a more thorough knowledge of guns, gun safety, and whatnot. I'm not inclined to do so, though. After all, I've got all these to-do lists to get through.

Ink in the Clink

Over the summer, my husband, "Captain Fun", had the idea for us to go visit a local music festival at The Ohio State Reformatory. I had just spent the weekend cooking and feeding a house full of people. I was ready to be off duty. "Sure!" I thought. "I'd rather go to prison than cook or clean one more thing."

The Ohio State Reformatory, not too far from our farm, is where the film *The Shawshank Redemption* was shot over 25 years ago. I loved that movie and was interested to see the building, a gothic-inspired kind of castle whose exterior beauty, I would find out, belies the sorrow within.

"A music festival out in the country ..." I mused. "Hmm ... what to wear?" We were just new to the area. I wanted to fit in out there, so I donned my cowgirl hat. It was a hot summer day, so a flouncy white skirt and light pink shirt were just the thing. "I wonder if there will be square dancing?" I thought.

Well, the "music festival" was titled "Ink in the Clink."

And it was a tattoo festival.

"Oh, okay, cool," I thought. Tattoos are so mainstream now. My daughter has a darling one on her foot. My hairdresser, a beautiful young woman whom I adore, rocks them all over her body, and she is precious. Tattoos are as ubiquitous as freckles these days. I'm not getting one, mind you, but I have no problem with them on other people. "Let's check it out."

At first, it felt like any other festival: corn dogs, elephant ears, fried cheese curds, freshly made lemonade ... all the usual suspects. But things took a dark turn fast when I turned the corner to the vendors' section. I knew I wasn't in Kansas anymore. First of all, I could not have felt more suburban, lily-white, middle-aged, square, and un-tatted. Everyone—and I mean everyone—was dressed in all black, goth attire—most with dyed black hair and sleeveless t-shirts. (Why have an arm tattoo if you're not going to show it off, right?) Nary a cowboy hat in sight. My flouncy white peasant skirt was like a beacon in a sea of darkness. I felt like a prison spotlight was following me throughout the festival, screaming, "Hey! I'm a big square, a poser, and I don't belong here! I'm not even a real farmer!"

I ventured in and swished over to check out the vendors. I noticed something swaying in the hot breeze ahead. "Oh, look! Is that some sort of wind chime?" Nope, it was an anatomically correct replica of an upside-down human being, skinned and hanging from a pole, swaying back and forth. "I don't need one of those, thanks," I whispered.

Onward. "Let's check out this toy booth. Looks like they have some cute teddy bears … oh no! Good God in heaven, what in the …?" There, before me, sat a disemboweled teddy bear. For sale. Apparently, there was a market for devil-faced teddy bears with their guts spilling out. They came in all sizes, too: large ones to put on grandma's rocking chair, medium-sized ones to give to the Munster kids, and tiny little ones to carry in one's purse, I guess. I backed away, trying not to show my revulsion, and walked over to check out the S&M whip and handcuff vendor next door. "I guess these go in the purse with the scary teddy," I thought.

"Babe, you want a beer?" my husband asked.

"Oh hell yeah." I wasn't (and still am not) a big fan of day drinking, but yes, I needed a very large can of beer. I was desperate to purge the image of the tortured teddy from my mind. "Let's go listen to the band," I said, guzzling my Natty Light.

I was expecting some good country music. Wrong again. The featured band, Saliva, was just starting. "Hmm. I'm not familiar with them," I thought, wiping beer from my mouth. (Now, I hate to sound as suburban, lily-white, middle-aged, square, and un-tatted as I am but, well, let's just say that Saliva was not my cup of drool.) I have no idea what the "singer" was saying, but I think he was very angry about something. Maybe he was scared of that devil teddy.

We downed the cold beers and went inside the Reformatory to check out the "ink" portion of the festival.

The interior of The Ohio State Reformatory is rather interesting and historical but oppressively sad. One can just feel the misery. It permeates the walls. Oh, and it's definitely haunted. (They have regular ghost hunting events, and I am 100% sure they bump into plenty.)

We perused the exhibits a bit then wandered into the old infirmary of the prison, where the inking was taking place. It was such a surreal scene: rows and rows of gurneys were lined up with customers laying down, receiving their customized tattoos in the hushed, semi-light. It felt like that scene in *Gone With the Wind* when the camera pans out to the rows upon rows of soldiers being treated for gruesome injuries. But these people were quite cheerful, paying good money to be here, and seemed completely at ease in this haunted prison. And the art being made was quite beautiful, really.

To complete the scene, for some reason, there was a little display in the corner of the room with jars of potions as well as preserved newts, bats, and God knows what else with a very serious sign in front of them: "No photographs please." No photos needed. These images will haunt my dreams.

After a quick tour of the prison cells, stacked one on top of the other like sad shoeboxes, paint peeling, as if the walls themselves were weeping, it was time to go.

Ink in the Clink was definitely an experience. The visuals were something else. But the most surprising thing was that, to a person, every single individual I encountered was completely lovely, polite, and welcoming. Even the tortured teddy vendor. Go figure. Maybe they just were coveting my pasty Irish flesh as a canvas for their art. Maybe they were high on the eye of newt or something. Or maybe you just can't judge a tattooed book by its cover.

Paul Bunyan and Rogue Babies

One of my husband's favorite activities on the farm is driving a four-wheeler around the property with me, breathing in the country air, and being master of his domain. Invariably, this includes a drive along the creek that separates our horse farm from our neighbor's cattle farm. We "poser farmers" enjoy watching the cows as they munch their way across the landscape, occasionally moo-ing their disapproval as we whisk by.

Recently, on one such tour, we came across our neighbor, the owner of said cattle farm, out stomping along the creek bed. This fellow is a Massive man, burly and strong with a round, kind, face. He reminds me of Paul Bunyan because he's as big as, well, a blue ox. He was poking along the fence line with a long stick, seemingly searching for something.

"Howdy!" my husband called out. "You lose something?"

One of Paul Bunyan's newborn calves had gone missing, and Paul was set on finding him. It was a scorching hot day and the calf, born just the day before, could have been in real danger in the heat. The mama cow mooed her concern as she followed Paul Bunyan along the fence line, and he nonchalantly chatted with us, all the while poking in the grass along the creek bed. "Yeah, they do this sometimes," he drawled. "Just get curious about the world and wander off."

I had learned that to be true the previous summer when I was fascinated by one such wandering calf. This rogue calf, on a daily basis, insisted on sneaking under the hot wire electric fence on Paul Bunyan's property to wander onto our property to graze. There she was, every day, a few times a day, putzing around on our hillside, munching and enjoying the view. It made me giggle every time I saw her: defiant, independent, her own gal. And every day, a few times a day, Paul Bunyan would have to wrangle her back to the fold. What was a pain in the rear and a lot of work for him was pure entertainment for me (which is kind of a theme for my pseudo farm life).

Our little rogue gal eventually grew too big to sneak under the fence without getting zapped, and her wandering stopped.

So here was Paul Bunyan, a year later, searching for yet another rogue calf. My husband and Paul exchanged chatter about animal breeding and horse foals vs. cow calves and such. "Is it a male or a female?" I asked, trying lamely to contribute to a conversation about which I knew very little.

"Oh, it's a male" Paul said. "Males can be that way. The young males can be kind of big and stupid."

"Just like human males," I replied. "They can be big and stupid, too." My gaze lifted to take in Paul Bunyan's Massive form. Our eyes met for an instant, and I realized I had just stepped in it.

Paul Bunyan let out a hearty laugh. "I guess I left myself open for that one!" he chortled as he walked on through the brush.

I let out a breath and laughed too. What a moron I am.

Paul Bunyan strolled on a bit, and we rode alongside until he found his rogue calf. There was Little Guy, in the heat of the day, lolling in the creek bed, cool water trickling past his tiny form. "Oh my!" I gasped. "Is he okay?"

"Oh, he's fine," Paul said. "He's just cooling off." The water must have felt fantastic on Little Guy, because when Paul went to grab him, he didn't even rustle. He just lay there like a nonviolent peace protestor. Paul scooped him up with one Massive arm, like the calf was a bundle of twigs, not a 100-pound animal, palming the calf under his soft, wet belly and carrying him up the creek bed. When he tried to set him down, Little Guy's legs were like a puppet's, lightly dangling on the ground under him. So, Paul tucked Little Guy gingerly under the hot wire fence and gently scooched him toward his mother. Mrs. Cow still watched the whole thing along the fence line, mooing her approval to Paul and, I would guess, chastising Little Guy for wandering so far and giving her such a fright.

Once on the other side of the fence, Little Guy finally found his legs and scampered up the hill, Mrs. Cow nudging him from behind. We drove away, waving goodbye to Paul Bunyan as he lumbered up the hill. And there they were, Mrs. Cow and Little Guy, reunited. Little Guy was hungrily nursing. All was forgiven.

Years ago, I had a toddler that was forever going rogue, only it involved her streaking down our suburban street naked after bath time, more times than I can count. I sympathized with that mommy cow's exasperation, anger ... and then relief and comfort.

Oh ... Deer

I spent most of the summers in my youth outdoors either weeding for my father or trying to avoid doing so by hiding from him in the woods behind our house. In all those formative years, I rarely—if ever—saw a deer in our neighborhood, in the woods behind our house, in the Metroparks nearby, or even on road trips to the West Virginia resort my family would visit every year. The closest I ever came to a deer was watching *Bambi* on Sunday nights after bath time.

Today, it's a different story. Deer are omnipresent. They are as commonplace as squirrels and way, way more obnoxious. When I'm working in the garden in my suburban backyard, I will often scare one up, waking her from her comfortable nap in my hostas. She will slowly get up and stroll away, surely muttering obscenities to me under her breath. She and her deer buddies in our neighborhood are like a marauding gang, roaming around with impunity—thuggish and ballsy. They just don't give a damn. When they cross a street, they seem to purposely take their time doing so.

"Yeah, I'm strolling across this major thoroughfare, stopping traffic both ways. And you're just going to sit there in your minivan and take it, lady," they scoff at me.

And they're a randy bunch, procreating with abandon. Every time I turn around there's another newborn fawn all curled up and cozy in someone's front yard.

When I'm cooking on the grill in my suburban backyard, a deer will stand there, chewing and staring at me blankly. "Um, Mar," one might say. "Those burgers seem to be overdone. And while we're talking about food ... you really need to plant more pansies in the front yard. I started nibbling on them this morning, and before I knew it, I had eaten the whole bed. They are like potato chips ... you can't have just one. Anyway, you're going to want to plant more pansies."

Last week on our annual family vacation in West Virginia, I witnessed a flock of fools hand-feeding a veritable herd of urban deer. It was like a Disney World character autograph scrum.

"Here, Bambi! Have some Cap'n Crunch," I thought I heard someone say.

"Why, thank you kind, simple tourist. And for your troubles, I will in turn give you some ticks with Lyme disease," the deer might say.

The sad truth is that these suburban deer are eating everything in their path because they're starving. The combination of urban sprawl and deer's propensity to reproduce faster than post-war Catholics is giving us deer that are too skinny and unhealthy. (Those deer on the resort hilltop were like ghostly apparitions.) Honestly, there are just too damned many deer for urban environments to sustain. Or West Virginia resorts, for that matter.

Out in the country around our farm, however, deer are deer. They are muscular and majestic because they are fit and living like wild animals, not pathetic circus sideshow acts. They are beautiful, really, just like the great prince of the forest, Bambi's father. They are appropriately skittish and mostly keep away from humans because they have gotten the message that humans out there in the country are often packing heat; they and their deer friends just might end up on someone's wall or dinner plate. But the result is that the deer population is under control. They are not overrunning the area, and there is enough vegetation for them to live healthy, happy lives. Out there, I don't hate deer.

My husband loves deer. In fact, he went so far as to plant apple trees on our farm so that they could treat themselves as they passed through our property. "Oh, that's so sweet!" I exclaimed. "What a nice thing to do for them."

"Yeah," he nodded. "It's going to make for a great deer hunting season."

It made me sad.

But then I thought of those ghostly deer on the hilltop or the Sharks and Jets-like deer gangs in our neighborhood back home. I'm no hunter, have no interest personally in killing deer, and am not fond of venison. But seeing firsthand the difference between healthy deer and sickly deer, I've come to the realization that hunting deer is a necessary part of keeping nature natural and the deer population as a whole healthy.

I know Bambi's mother was taken out by a deer hunter, and that broke my little heart. (Don't all Disney mothers find tragic, untimely ends?) But isn't it also heartbreaking to see a once majestic beast reduced to eating boxed cereal out of a human's hand?

Joan Crawford, Dennis, and Mr. Wilson

One of my favorite pastimes on our farm is observing the animals there. In doing so, I have learned that, while we humans can idealize animals as being kinder and more decent than the human race, that is not always the case. Sometimes animals can be just as loathsome as we humans.

Our farm is a racehorse-breeding business where owners bring their female horses to our farm to be inseminated, gestate, and give birth under the knowing hand of Mark and his right-hand gal, Melinda.

About a year into our farm adventure, a mare came onto the property already pregnant. She gave birth according to plan and her little colt began nursing and thriving. Then the horse shit hit the fan. Mrs. Horse was clearly not right. Out of nowhere one day, she began beating up on her little colt. The foal, a colt they named Dennis, had scrapes and cuts inflicted by his nutty mom. It was emotional for the whole staff of the farm to witness. But Mark and his team knew that colt needed his mother's milk as long as possible in order to thrive, so they hesitantly left him with her a few more days … until it became obvious that the mare—we'll call her Joan Crawford—was a *Mommie Dearest* nightmare and had taken to trying to rip the hide off her colt. They finally separated them, sending Dennis to the animal hospital at The Ohio State University to recover from his wounds before he returned to the farm.

Enter: the companion goat. I've learned that occasionally this kind of thing can happen in horses, that the mother is just a bad seed and needs to be separated from her foal. While the foal can be supplemented with formula or granular milk, he still needs companionship to thrive, so horse farms will routinely bring in a companion goat. They will also do this if a mother horse dies in childbirth. The little goat's job is just to be a buddy, a wingman, a roommate. So, walking through the barns, one would pass the stalls and see a mama horse and filly, a mama horse and colt, a baby horse and … a goat. It's an unusual sight.

Dennis and the goat got along famously. They would nuzzle each other, run together out in the paddock, or—like old friends in a coffee shop—just munch their food silently next to one another. It was really sweet.

The staff grew to love that silly goat and named him Mr. Wilson as a nod to the character in the *Dennis the Menace* comic strip. Mr. Wilson acted like a playful dog, scampering around the barn, chasing the cats, peeking around the corners. He even figured out how to open his and Dennis' stall door, the little scamp.

But eventually, things took a dark turn. One misty morning, Mark entered the barn to start the day's chores and witnessed a disturbing thing. Dennis was abusing Mr. Wilson, just as his own mother had abused him. Again, it was shocking, and heartbreaking. Mark and his staff had worked so hard to nurse that colt back to health, to make him feel loved and nurtured. And poor Mr. Wilson. He must have been equally disillusioned. "Dude, I'm on your side," he must have thought. "What the farm?" And so, to the sadness of all, Mr. Wilson went back to his original owner.

Dennis lived alone in his stall, growing bigger and more combative every day. When all the other foals were eventually weaned from their own mothers, all the colts were put in the same paddock. Dennis was by far the biggest and meanest of them all. The other colts instinctively knew something was off with Dennis and took turns going at him, kicking him, and generally bullying him. It was like a very rough schoolyard scene, and it helped make Dennis a badass, a thug. It was sad, really. Dennis didn't have a chance.

Joan Crawford wasn't popular in the fields after the separation either. The other mama horses kept her at bay on the outskirts of their circles. They knew she wasn't right. Eventually, Joan's owner sold her at an auction with the caveat that she never be bred again because, clearly, girlfriend couldn't be trusted as a mom. The day she was sent to auction, her paperwork was out of order; she had to return to the farm for a few days. When she was put back into the field with the other mares, there was a tense scene. One by one, each of the five or six mares in that field charged up to Joan, kicking and braying, as if to say, "Aw, hell no, Joan Crawford! You hurt your baby, and we all know it, you bitch. You are not welcome here." That display continued for a couple of days until Joan Crawford finally left the farm for good, and calm returned.

I'm sure Dennis went on to be a big, mean successful racehorse. And hopefully, Joan Crawford is living a peaceful existence pulling an Amish plow somewhere, thinking about the error of her ways.

Was Joan abused as a foal? Was this learned behavior? Perhaps some combination of both? Who knows, but the whole cycle of abuse and nature vs. nurture was as distressing as it was interesting.

Life has gone on at the farm with dozens of foals being born and raised without incident each year since Dennis and Joan Crawford left. Watching the good moms devotedly tend to their young each season is a beautiful sight and often makes me think of my own mom; of being a mom myself; and how blessed I have been to have an excellent mother, good role models, a safe upbringing, and good genes. In life and on horse farms, that should never be taken for granted.

Captain Fun's Wild Ride

He dashes through the woods on a four-wheeler, his passengers being tossed to and fro like rag dolls. He conquers the hilly terrain like a seasoned pro, expertly maneuvering his vehicle as it fishtails in the slippery mud. He whips up hills and down dales at lightning speeds, stopping only to survey his acreage, his deer stands and of course, his magnificent home on the hill. He is "Captain Fun". And when people visit, they will experience his wild ride.

My husband, "Captain Fun", is a busy bee when we're on our farm property. There's walking the dog; toting the garbage to the bin; staring at the horses, trees, and hillsides; the stroking of the beard. And, when we have guests, there's the task of taking them on *the ride*. And it's epic.

"Hey, who wants to go for a little ride?" he asks. Everyone jumps up enthusiastically, anxious to get a look at our beautiful surroundings. Our guests enter the Kubota four-wheeler, a very capable little tank of a four-wheel drive, open-air vehicle, naively expecting a quick little tour of the property. It begins innocently enough … "There's the horses, most of them are pregnant … there's the neighbor's property and their cows … there's more cows, more horses." Then it gets interesting. Like a flash, "Captain Fun" switches the vehicle into four-wheel drive and we dart up into the woods.

He loves this part because our guests never see it coming. Up, up, up we climb into the woods.

In the middle of the summer, the undergrowth and brush are thick as a rainforest. Birds are squawking, winging out of our way. Squirrels, deer, foxes, and such run for cover. "Captain Fun" navigates up the path, vines, brambles, and branches whipping the legs and arms of those sitting on the outside edges of the vehicle. There are screams from the back seat. It's like a more thrilling version of a ride in "Frontier Town" at an amusement park, without the hokey animated cowboys and Indians. "Argh!" they laugh/scream. "Is this safe?"

We come across a rocky stream. Will "Captain Fun" be daunted? Hell no. He charges headlong through the stream, water splattering us all, that amazing vehicle grinding through the muck. Sometimes we slow down, our Captain easing us over a boulder or a fallen tree. And just when you think, "Damn, I shouldn't have worn slippers for this ride. It looks like we're hoofing it through the mud back to the house," he expertly pulls us all through the hazard like a seasoned African safari guide.

For a hot second, we emerge from the woods out into a field of corn or soybeans or timothy (that's a kind of grass that's especially nutritious for farm animals). The Captain will take the four-wheeler out into the field, crunching down the edges of whatever is growing there under our wheels as we whiz into the woods again, careening down slippery slopes, our guests shrieking in the back seat, "Oh my gaawwwd!" which only makes The Captain press down the pedal harder. We will stop for a moment as he hops out of the vehicle and checks on his "critter cam," a motion-activated camera he and his buddy set up in the woods to keep an eye out for … I'm not exactly sure what. Then he hops back behind the wheel, and we're off again.

Finally, we are spit out onto the level ground of the gravel driveway and head back to the house. We hear laughing from the back seat. "Holy crap! What was that?!" There's relief in their voices, as if they just went through the looking glass to some otherworld and are glad to be back in civilization. But they love it … after it's over.

"Captain Fun" loves it, too. Sure, he's energized by their screams of terror and delight, but he also just loves showing off his farm and the beauty it holds. He loves sharing stories of all that he's learned, of how this farm seemed to just drop down from heaven into his lap. Okay, and he loves showing off his four-wheeler skills.

After "Captain Fun"'s wild rides, we usually end up in front of the fireplace in the winter or out on the deck in the summer, reliving the ride, laughing hysterically at each other's reactions to the unexpected brushes with death (not really, but it feels like it at the time). The Captain will pop the "critter cam" drive into his laptop, and we'll all gather around to see what secrets it holds. "Yep, there's a squirrel … there's another. Oh, wait, there's a deer … there's another." It's riveting stuff.

"Oh, look! What's that blurry image caught whizzing by?" It's none other than "Captain Fun" himself, caught on his own critter cam, on another ride with other unsuspecting guests, gripping the edges of their seats with looks of terror in their eyes.

We pick thorns and pricklers out of each other's hair and clothes, sometimes putting bandages on some bloody scratches on legs or forearms. And then, we toast the farm, life, and—much to his delight—we turn and toast "Captain Fun".

How We Got Our Cement Pond

Shortly after my husband and I purchased our farm, we were coming back from a hot hike around the property and I said, "Wow, wouldn't a pool be great out here?" He chuckled and dismissed me out of hand.

A little while later, my husband and his buddy, who had a gorgeous garden of his own, took a weekend to plan and plant our first garden. It was a sight to behold: organized rows labeled with "lettuce," "eggplant," "beans," etc. But untended gardens are prone to weeds, and while we were away from the farm for a couple of weeks, our beautifully planted garden became overrun and was barely recognizable.

"We're going to have to get up early to weed that garden tomorrow," I warned. "Before the heat of the day."

"Yeah, sure," my husband replied, tapping on his laptop.

Morning came, and again I declared, "We'd better get going out there while the ground is still soft and get those weeds out."

"Okay," he replied, closing the bathroom door behind him.

"I know your game, Tom Sawyer," I thought. "You're waiting for me to do it myself and then you will waltz in at the end and tell me what a good job I've done. Not this time, pal. I am not weeding that whole garden alone." And so, I waited. And waited.

Finally, he stirred, and sure enough, there we were in the heat of the midday sun, bent over picking weeds. And, just as I had warned, they weren't coming out. The tops of the weeds would pop off, leaving the roots in place. Under the blazing sun, one by one, the blasted weeds held fast to the earth.

Finally, he stood up, arms akimbo, looking like an irritated Jolly Green Giant. As the heat seared us both, he wiped his brow and surveyed the situation. "Screw this," he declared. "Let's put a pool here." He threw down his garden gloves and walked away.

And that's how we came to have a pool at our farm.

Swimming in that pool now, I can feel my mother, Marge's, approval. She loved the water, even though she didn't learn to swim until she was in her 50s. She and I would go to my cousin's above-ground pool in the summer where she and her sister, donning those goofy floral bathing caps, would stand in the middle of the pool, just smoothing the water with their fingertips in circles around them. They chatted about their respective families, their brood of children, and who knows what else. I was busy bobbing up and down nearby, like a seal pup near its mother.

When Marge finally did learn to swim, she had a classic swimming move: the sidestroke. I've never seen anyone else do it, but it was the perfect way for a gal to get from one end of the pool to the other without getting her face wet or ruining her coiffed hair. It looked like a movie of Esther Williams, the swimming movie star of the '40s whom my mother was said to resemble in her youth. Marge would keep her head above water the whole time and reach one arm forward, then the other, but never turn her body. All she needed was musical accompaniment and maybe some leg kicks and it would have been water ballet.

Marge would love this farm pool because she also loved horses. In this pool, she would be able to sidestroke over to the edge and watch as mares and foals graze and stroll in the grassy fields below. I can just hear her saying in awe, "Aren't they magnificent animals?"

One of the last-minute additions to the pool project was an outdoor shower. I floated that idea early on and got it shot down ... but guess who is wild about the outdoor shower now? My husband will tell anyone who will listen about how he loves that shower. Can't blame him. There's something about showering in the out of doors. It's so refreshing and liberating. And it feels slightly naughty. ("I'm naked. Outside!" I always think to myself). Between the pool and the shower, it's a freaking farm fantasy.

My husband's high noon decision a few years back to get a pool at the farm was a good one (as well as the audible call on the shower). And we still do have that garden as well. After working in the garden or going on a hot walk, there's nothing better than taking a "Nestea plunge" in that cement pond. But I know that deep down, my husband's decision on the pool was all about making this place a gathering spot for family and friends as well as sweetening the pie for our girls. It was all about making this farm more desirable for them as they travel far and wide in their respective lives: something to keep them coming home, maybe someday with families of their own. I'm not in a hurry for that stage in life, but when it comes, I look forward to teaching the next generation "the smooth," and the sidestroke, courtesy of Marge/Esther Williams.

Zen and the Art of Mowing

As anyone who has driven on an interstate highway knows, Ohio has a lot of corn. While some find it monotonous, I have fallen in love with the sight of vast fields of corn—waves of corn—undulating in the hot summer breeze in a beautiful, bucolic ballet. Driving down country roads, I am always reminded of the line "amber waves of grain" from the song, "America the Beautiful." Except, these are emerald waves of corn.

Little known fact: corn is a relative of grass. Looking out from the deck of our farmhouse, we see a vast field of corn and its cousin, grass. A lot of grass. The horses grazing on it are in heaven this time of year, enjoying its sweet, juicy nutrients. Farm manager, Mark and his staff are meticulous keepers of the grass. If they were in the suburbs, they'd be one of those families who win the Lawn Olympics on their cul-de-sac. But out here, they're not out to impress anyone. They just have impeccable standards, a beautiful aesthetic. And they love to cut grass.

Farm work is unending; every day there are dozens of things to get done before noon, not the least of which is keeping many animals alive each day. One of Mark's favorite escapes is hopping on a riding mower and setting out to cut the acres and acres of grass. He straps on the goggles and ear protectors with built-in speakers for music, fires up the machine, and off he goes … steadily riding up and over the hills, occasionally doing a nifty twirl around a tree or a rock. It is a sight to behold. He is a master, painstakingly going over the grass as if it is a sand Zen garden, creating neat, green stripes on the hillsides. It must be very satisfying. Unlike waiting over ten months for a horse to foal, this offers immediate gratification. When he's finished, the hills stand as a testament to a job well done.

I see all those acres of grass and remember my dad surveying his acre of suburban paradise. I can still smell that freshly cut grass and hear the quiet hiss and click, click, click of the sprinkler. He loved pushing his power mower back and forth for much the same reasons, I imagine: an escape from kids, clients, everything.

It was like meditation for him, a prayer. He never got a riding mower, though salespeople over the years tried to convince him. He liked the exercise that pushing a mower gave him. As he grew older, he would sit on his green string chaise lounge and admire his sons and then grandsons pushing his mower for him. He had passed the grass-cutting baton to them, but reluctantly. Nothing pleased him more than cutting the grass, then reclining to admire his work as he sipped hot tea on a sweltering summer afternoon and watched the sprinkler baptize his lawn.

I never got to cut the grass. I was always in charge of weeding the grass … and the flowerbeds … and anything else with roots.

When my husband and I got married and bought our first house, it came with a lawnmower. He handled the lawn mowing for a hot second but quickly grew tired of it. Watching the jungle grow in front of my house, I took the reins one day. "How hard could this be?" I asked myself, lathering up with sunscreen.

Back and forth I went on our little plot of suburban land. Easy enough. But when I finished, I looked back and noticed there were little mohawk tufts of grass between my newly cut rows. It seemed I didn't line up the lawnmower correctly in my back-and-forth march across the yard. So, I started to re-cut the grass, slicing down the mohawk tufts. But now the grass was uneven, so I darted from spot to spot, slicing down any irregularities. Pretty soon, I found myself in the middle of the front yard, moving the lawnmower back and forth outward like it was a vacuum. I formed a weird kind of sunflower pattern on the lawn. "This is harder than I thought," I muttered to myself, sweat dripping from my chins. "How did I lose control like this?"

Just then, a grandmother and her grandbaby in a stroller walked down from the corner and stopped in front of my house. "We've been watching you from down the street and just had to come closer. This is the funniest thing I've ever seen. Please go on."

"Glad to amuse you, ma'am!" I hollered over the lawnmower's buzz. What an exasperating exercise. That's the last time I mowed a lawn.

The grass around that house was often too long. My husband would occasionally try to tackle it in the little free time he had as a young entrepreneur. More often than not, he would recruit a willing teenager in the neighborhood to do it for us.

When we bought our forever house several years later, it had a yard twice the size. When packing up to move, my husband gave the mower away. "I'm done with that crap," he said. "I'm paying someone else to do it."

Now we have farm property with acres and acres of grassy land. And, we have the mother of all riding mowers. Mark won't allow my husband to ride it yet, though. With all those hills and fancy swivel gears on the machine, it's a bit more complicated than pushing a mower back and forth. And for anyone who doesn't know what he's doing (say, us) it could be downright dangerous. Large farm equipment, sexy as it is, is not to be trifled with.

"I'm going to ride that thing someday," my husband vows, gazing longingly at the Zen master Mark, riding up and down the hillsides. I chuckle to myself every time he says it, amused by the irony. Funny how life works. I guess he was just waiting for the right kind of grass and the right kind of mower. Timing is everything.

County Fair

Today we went to a county fair just south of our farm property. It was a perfect day for a county fair: overcast, breezy, not too hot. We wandered through the back roads, searching for signs of the fair. All of the sudden, there it was, nestled amidst rolling farmland.

This being my first county fair, I wasn't exactly sure what to expect. At first, it was pretty much just like the carnival that comes to my suburban town. There was fried food of all sorts—fried pickles, fried elephant ears, fried hot dogs on a stick, cheese on a stick, French fries and more—as well as rickety fair rides that encourage the spewing of all the aforementioned fried foods.

But as we continued, it struck me that, no, this was not really like my suburban carnival. Folks were milling about going to and from different barns filled with animals large and small. Most folks were wearing high rubber boots. While some of us in the suburbs wear overpriced rubber boots to be darling and skip through the city puddles, these people—authentic farmers—were wearing those boots for real. They keep one's feet clean and dry when shoveling shit out of a barn stall. Same thing with the cowboy boots. They do a fine job keeping their wearer's toes uncrushed by horses.

I usually only see cowboy boots on young people when I go to, say, a Zac Brown Band concert at Blossom Music Center, an outdoor venue in our area. There, all sorts of sometimes-y cowgirls in cheeky Daisy Duke shorts and straw cowboy hats swill boozy concoctions that end up being puked all down their cropped shirts by the end of the concert.

Wandering aimlessly through the fair, we wove in and out of various animal barns. First, we moseyed into the rabbit barn where a dozen or so middle schoolers were prepping their rabbits to be judged. I have no idea what the judges were looking for; they all looked like fine rabbits to me. But the young people were earnestly cradling their animals with such pride and anticipation. It was moving.

I was rooting for the grayish-brown one because it looked like my pet rabbit from my youth, Brandy (named after that one-hit-wonder by the '70s band, Looking Glass). Poor Brandy bit it when I was about eight-years-old after she snuck into the garage and feasted on fertilizer. Brandy met a better end than my previous pet rabbit, Puff, a little black beauty. Puff went "poof" when I mistakenly left her out all night, tethered to her cage; a raccoon—or something—decided to eat her for dinner. I don't know the details of what happened to my first rabbit, Oreo, a black and white little number. But she, too, met an untimely, violent death.

So, I enjoyed my visit in the rabbit barn, but didn't stay long. I didn't want my bad rabbit luck to impact them.

On to the sheep and llama barn. There, too, were earnest young people dutifully washing and showering their sheep, combing their llamas, lovingly getting ready to show off the hard work they had put into raising their respective animals. It was a pretty chilly day and all the sheep had just been shorn, so they were wearing little jackets, some with hoodies. They all lounged about as if they were in a spa, just lazing on the straw, waiting for their next treatment. I think one was reading *The National Enquirer*.

Our next stop was the poultry barn. No lazing there. Lots of clucking and fussing, feathers all ruffled. I was surprised by the variety of chickens there: black and white striped with shocking red heads, gray elegant plumage with just a splash of red atop the head, beautiful russets with amber highlights like a professionally done balayage from a salon. (I think I had that last color in the '90s.) There were also many varieties of turkey there, including a few enormous, fluffy, white fellas that filled their cages such that their feathers spilled out from the tops and sides.

Walking down the midway, I noticed a chance to ride a mechanical bull. "No, thanks," I thought. It's all fun and games until you can't move your extremities.

We continued on, sweeping through the small animal barn, which featured a variety of goats that were very restless, as goats generally are. They were all chewing on their stalls and trying to climb out.

After all those small animals, it was time for the bigguns: the heifers and milk cows. These beasts were beauts. Each was impeccably washed, groomed, and spit-shined, like pieces of farm art. I wanted to take one home for the living room.

The most exciting visit was to the swine barn. These pigs were also Massive. Again, many were just lying around, bored and looking very, very full. Some were so hefty that, lying on their sides, their rotund girths forced their legs to jut out straight so that their hooves didn't even touch the ground. (That's a lot of pig.) At one point, several pigs were being showered and gussied up at the end of the alleyway of stalls. After their grooming, they were rushed down the path by their young owners, being herded with a little stick. One large fella broke free and was running rogue all through the barn. Startled and a little scared, I had to hop to the side to keep from being knocked over by that fat pig. I'm not sure where he was rushing to … maybe home again, home again, jiggity jig?

Next door to the hogs were the horses, and they were impressive. Enormous. Some had withers that were taller than I, and I'm pretty tall. A blue-ribbon winning draft horse was out front of the horse barn, gathering accolades and nose pets. She was Massive, black and shiny, with delicate pink ribbons down her mane. Her owner, a young woman of about 18 or so, beamed with pride like a stage mother at a kiddy beauty pageant.

Before leaving, we stopped into the awards tent. All manner of pickles, pies, quilts, and such were on display, bedecked with blue ribbons and the names of people I didn't know, but wished I did. I could tell that each entry was crafted with care and pride, just like those animals in the barns around us. It looked like Charlene Butina swept the field in the "Golden Age" category for anything pickled as did Susan Faulker in the "Adult" category. Judy Golas killed it in the "Golden Age" category for quilting. My heart swelled with pride and admiration for these strangers. "Atta way, ladies," I thought to myself, running my fingers over the blue ribbons.

Our farm is right on the Richland County border with Knox County, nearby Ashland County, which means there are plenty of county fairs in our future. And I have to say, I'm looking forward to seeing how they compare to each other. It's all so old school. Not computer generated, contrived, or pretentious. Honest to God, it's good for the soul. I am clearly an interloper, a farm life voyeur, but I left the Knox County Fair that day downright inspired.

The Gift of a Good Nap

After a morning of hot, sticky, 4th of July festivities in our farm town that were cut short by a thunderstorm, we all scampered home. My sister Susan and I relaxed on the porch to the sounds of a soft rain. Pretty soon, we both were slack-jawed, heads back, overcome by sleep. The rain drizzled outside, gently tap-tapping the tree leaves close by. Every now and then, my sister was startled awake by the sounds of a cow mooing nearby. "It's okay, it's just a cow," I whispered to her as she drifted back into slumber. (You don't hear that in the suburbs.)

Then a few days later, rain again softly falling, I set up my nook on the porch with reading and writing supplies and some hot herbal tea. The wind began to swish through the trees, sending the leaves of the tulip tree next to our porch into a hushed frenzy. Puffs of air moved the wind chimes into a low, long, bonging song. And the subtle hiss of a light rain enveloped me into squishy slumber. What a gift: a twenty-minute, total surrender into tranquility. A nap.

My mother was the supreme queen of all nappers. With a chaotic house full of kids, she always prioritized her naptime. She used to say, "You can handle anything in life if you have your sleep." And, "You know, they use sleep deprivation as a torture technique. You have to get your sleep."

As a little girl and all the way into high school, I would come home after school just as my mom was waking from her afternoon nap. I'd climb into bed next to her, and we would both lie on our backs and sing, talk, and laugh about who was the latest guest on *The Dinah Shore Show, The Merv Griffin Show* or *The Tonight Show with Johnny Carson.* "That Paul Lynde, what a cutup," she'd say. Or, "What is with that Charo and the 'cuchi, cuchi'?" And after a beat of quiet, laying there, staring at the ceiling, our legs tented side-by-side, "Why is Orson Welles famous anyways?"

When I was very little, Mom would roll over onto her stomach and have me walk on her back like one of those yoga goats. Balancing myself by pressing my hands flat onto the ceiling, my dirty feet would pad over her soft, pillowy back, and she would groan with relief. That was always followed by a scratching session with me using my scraggly fingernails, looking for her "spot"—that part of her back that she could never reach but always bothered her.

Lying down on another Saturday afternoon at our farm after a particularly busy week back home, I try to get into the nap zone and breathe to clear out my monkey brain. I have my sister on my mind. It's been a week filled with heavy-hearted tasks and decisions, helping care for Susan as she had slipped further into Alzheimer's Disease. I try using some yoga meditations, visualizing sunsets, or just listening to the sound of silence to no avail.

Susan's gift as her disease progresses is that she has been able to nap every day, escaping the stress of coping with her ever-changing reality. I think of my mom, who went through the same arduous, tragic decline but also held onto her napping prowess. I hold them both in my heart as I worry, pray and try to let go of it all to sleep a spell … but there will be no napping today.

I Am Starlight

Late summer is time for the Perseid meteor shower. I always forget about it, and so every August, it is a pleasant surprise.

I recently had a group of gal pals out at the farm for an overnight get-together. After we had supped, laughed, and told stories by candlelight inside, we adjourned to the deck with blankets and herbal tea. We leaned back to take in the late evening whilst talking, staring at the starry sky. Every so often, a lone satellite silently traveling above broke the stillness of the dotted dome. A couple of red-eye flight airplanes appeared, noiselessly ferrying folks from one side of the continent to another. The cell towers in the distance stood sentry, beeping their red lights, reminding us that the outside world was still there. As our eyes adjusted to the darkness, we were startled and delighted to find nature's fireworks coming into focus.

"So, I'm getting ready for another thirteen-hour college trip at the end of the month," I was saying to no one in particular. "My ass hurts just thinking … Ohhhhh my God!" The light show had begun.

When I see a shooting star, I just can't help it. I start screaming. And laughing. It's always so surprising. I'm just staring at a silent sky one minute, and the next, it comes alive.

"Holy cow!" I kept scream/laughing. "Woo hoo!"

I finally settled down, returning to our conversation. "I totally hate my bedroom. I feel like we are sleeping in a guy's dorm room. I mean, we've been married for almost 30 years. It is time to … Holy crap! There goes another one!"

It went on like this for a couple of hours, chatter interrupted by my screaming and laughing. It was delightful. Eventually, we all turned in, one by one, letting the light show go on without us.

The next day, I hugged my pals goodbye and retreated to the house alone, with the dog. I puttered around, did some work on my computer, and then noticed the sun setting. I grabbed a glass of wine and some leftovers and had a silent dinner outside, listening to the sounds of late summer, cicada songs filling the air with their cree-cree-cree-creeeeeee.

The sunset threw purple and yellow colors all over the clouds as the birds swooped and chatted to each other to settle down for the night. After taking the four-wheeler for a drive, chasing the fading light, I returned to my perch on the deck to look for an encore of the previous night's light show.

It was a slow night in the heavens, though. The Perseid shower was down to a drip.

Gazing upward, my mind drifted, and I remembered being a 10-year-old girl, looking out my parents' TV room window at the stars above. I was an awkward, chubby 10-year-old, in a stage my mother would describe as "betwixt and between:" still a child but wanting to be older, cooler, prettier. I felt compelled to wish on the first star of the night—out loud. "Starlight, star bright, first star I see tonight. I wish I may, I wish I might. Have the wish I wish tonight." What was I wishing for so earnestly? Probably a boyfriend. Or boobs. Or tan skin. Or for my older brothers to be nice to me. Or for a princess phone in my room like my friend Maureen.

Unfortunately, there was no such thing as privacy in our house. One of my brother's darling friends was there and overheard me. I had a wild crush on this friend. He had a John Travolta kind of handsomeness (Travolta from the '70s, not the creepy vibe he's rocking these days) with a wealth of wavy, dark hair and a strong jaw. "John Travolta" laughed out loud at me.

"Are you wishing on a star?" he chortled.

"No, I'm …." I mumbled as I retreated, my face turning a hot red.

"Awww. You're so cute. Starlight, star bright ..." he semi-mocked.

I was mortified. I wanted to die, to disappear, to vaporize.

And yet, he *had* just talked to me. And he did think I was cute. In a pathetic way, but still. I would take whatever crumbs he'd give me.

For years and years after that, "John Travolta" would bound into my mom's house and always, always give me a, "Hey, Starlight. How's it going?" as he went upstairs to my brother's room.

I chuckled to myself on my farm deck, alone with my dog, staring upward. Remembering the John Travolta look-alike, my wish on the star that evening, my utter embarrassment, and also my thrill at having been noticed by a boy.

I'm a grown ass adult now. I did eventually get boobs, date boys, even married one. And somewhere in my late teens, I think my brothers started to actually like me. Never did get that princess phone, though.

I was starting to pack up my blanket and my empty wine glass when one last, dramatic salutation from above bid me good night. A giant, thick shooting star etched its way across the sky, looking for all the world like a streak of white chalk arcing across a big celestial blackboard.

"Whoa!" I laughed out loud to myself. "That was awesome!"

I quickly made a wish that I would never tire of seeing that kind of thing.

Rolling on the River

Our farm property in mid-Ohio is close to one of the area's most beautiful and popular refuges: Mohican State Park. Loudonville, Ohio boasts gorgeous stands of towering pine trees; stretches of hiking and horseback riding trails; and miles of winding creeks and rivers, the most popular of which is the Black Fork Mohican River, home to Mohican Adventures.

During one of our first summers with the farm in our lives, my husband and I booked a river rafting adventure. This was a popular spot for school and scouting field trips. I had not been there since a 3.2 beer-soaked afternoon in high school back in 1982; I was excited to go back. Our youngest daughter, Rose, came with us—under duress. Her high school classmates who were supposed to come out to the farm for the weekend canceled on her at the last minute, and we forced her to accompany us anyway because, you know, we are awful parents.

"This will be fun!" I cajoled her as I packed our things. "It's a nice hot day, and the river will be quiet and cool. It will be so relaxing to be out in nature."

I just didn't count on all the people who were thinking the same thing.

The canoe livery was a bustling place that smelled like a water ride at an amusement park and was populated with the same caliber of large-ish, t-shirted, sweaty patrons. These were in the days before COVID concerns, so we pushed our way into the crowd, trying on life jackets that smelled like dirty jockstraps, and plunked ourselves into the mud-smeared canoes. "See! Isn't this fun?" I cooed. Silence from Miss Rose.

As we pushed out into the river, the slow current pulled us in. Boats full of young families and rowdy teenagers surrounded us, so we paddled away to find the serenity I was seeking. I had flashes of scenes from *Pocahontas* in my head as I stroked the water with my oar. My girls and I loved that movie when they were all young, with its soaring soundtrack and strong, beautiful heroine. I was imagining myself—a white, middle aged, decidedly non-Native American woman—with cartoonish, raven-colored hair; a winsome profile; and that enviable Disney princess 20" waistline, as I belted out,

"What I love most about rivers is
You can't step in the same river twice
The water's always changing, always flowing ..."

Rose stroked the water, staring blankly ahead.

I continued, "What's around the riverbend
Waiting just around the riverbend."

But after the first bend in the river, all I found was miles of RV and trailer park campgrounds, bustling with weekend partiers. It was 10:30 a.m. and I heard that familiar sound of a brewsky being cracked open on the riverside. A shirtless man sitting on a lawn chair rested the can on his generous girth as scores of children ran amok ... and I do mean muck. The riverbed was pretty low from the dry spring, giving the water the muddy look of a parking lot puddle. I waved a tepid hello. "Good morning!" He raised his beer to toast me.

"Can I squirt you, lady?" yelled a kid, crocodile-swimming toward our canoe through the shallow water. Other kids were running and swimming around, through and above the river as well. It was a *Lost Boys*-meets-*Lord of the Flies* kind of vibe.

"Oh, no, thanks," I replied as his less polite friend drenched Rose with a bazooka water soaker. We both were sticky with river mud already, so what did it matter, honestly? Except that Rose kept up her steely silence.

We continued on, meandering past more campgrounds full of volleyball nets, smoking grills, and homes that ranged from modest to extravagant. Some houses had folded lawn chairs; others were festooned with party lights. Some had painstakingly manicured landscaping while others had a couple of lonely flower pots. It was all very sweet, very mid-Ohio Americana. I felt like a voyeur, floating by a diorama of "Life in the Midwest, USA, summer 2000s."

We had just turned another river bend and were greeted by a raucous group of young men. And more brewskies. "Woo hoo! Show us your tits!" they screamed. Rose, repulsed, started stroking her oar faster. "Oh, no, not happening!" I yelled. " Just passing through!"

We were roughly midway through our journey, and navigating through that diorama had made us hungry. Luckily, the Mohican River is peppered with weird little float-up eateries serving burgers, fish and chips, chicken skewers, hot dogs, beverages … the works. There's even beer to-go. None of it felt very regulated or legal, but we had come this far.

"To hell with it. Let's do this." I said as I stroked toward the "Captain Weenie" vendor and ordered us all some hot dogs and beer.

Rose broke her silence to declare she "would rather starve to death."

She did have a point. There was something just not right about buying food made in a ramshackle houseboat, eating it in a filthy canoe whilst having swamp ass, and floating in muddy river water. We ate and drank just the same. But I checked that off my to-do list. Didn't need to do that again. Ever.

After our visit to mid-Ohio's version of the "wet market," we floated on to find what we came for: an open stretch of quiet woods. The revelers and beer swillers were left behind, the canoes were spread apart, and all there was to hear was the wind, the birds, and the splash of the oars. Dappled sunlight scattered in front of us, shining through leafy branches as the towering trees swayed in the breeze. And all of the sudden, it was smooth sailing.

It really was a lovely day. All of it. Even the amphibious float-through, marginally sanitary dining options.

I look back on that day and feel like it was a metaphor for times to come, the pandemic era, which followed several years later. 2020 felt very much like we all were paddling against the current, losing our oars, getting super-soaked with wretched, muddy river water, and putting up with unseemly behavior by way too many people.

Today, with those difficulties behind us, I'm hanging onto the hope that there is smooth water with quiet breezes ahead.

Just around the riverbend.

THE BEAUTIFUL MUNDANE: SEASONLESS STORIES

Let Sleeping Ghosts Lie

We have two pre-Civil War burial grounds on the property.
Reportedly there are 24 plots there, circa 1824. A descendant of the
buried contacted us asking permission to find one of the cemeteries
in order to locate their ancestors' headstones. When I first heard
this, I initially thought, "Sure, what harm would it do? What could
happen?"

And then I remembered every scary movie ever and thought, "Oh,
hell no." I've seen the movie *Poltergeist* (through the fingers over my
eyes). Bad things happen when you mess with graveyards. And I can
barely tolerate ghost stories.

Several years ago, we went on a wonderful trip to Ireland. The Irish
know their ghosts. Tales abound over there about "the banshee."
With its sad, tortured history, one can just feel ghosts are everywhere.
We were traveling with a group of eleven family members and were
staying in the famous Ashford Castle in County Mayo for one night.
After dinner, our waiter asked if we would like a ghost tour of the
castle. As I shook my head "no," the rest of the table all chimed in
with a "yes!" Not wanting to be alone in my room in a haunted castle,
I agreed to go.

Our charming waiter took us up back stairways and hidden rooms.
At one point, he notified us that the hallway we were entering was
colder than the rest of the house. This indicated that there was
paranormal activity there. The group of us huddled together like a
well-dressed scrum as the waiter showed us secret doors and creepy
portraits, including one of a young girl, all dressed in white, who died
young. He said she still walked the halls at night. "You will know her
by a white wisp in the air," he said. I snapped photos of this and that,
staying in the middle of the scrum, lest a banshee reach out and grab
me.

That night, of course I did not sleep at all. I listened to the sounds of the 800-year-old building, hoping my husband's snoring would scare away any ghostly little girls. I had to pee but dared not attempt the journey to the bathroom alone. When my husband got up to use the loo around 2 a.m., I leapt out of bed to join him, sticking to his back like a shadow, scaring him in the process. "What the hell are you doing?" he barked.

"I'm afraid of that blasted little girl ghost!", I cried, doing a dance to hold in my pee. I made him wait for me before he went back to bed.

Morning finally came, and the eleven of us were bleary-eyed as we shuffled onto our little bus. (It seemed no one else had slept either.) As I took my perch in the front of the bus, I opened my phone and started scanning photos of the day before. When I came to the photos of the ghost tour, my heart skipped a beat. It seems that when I snapped a pic of the chilly "paranormal" hallway, I may have captured that ghostly little girl in the form of a "white wisp in the air." I passed the photo around to see if everyone else saw the same thing I saw. One by one, everyone stared at the photo in a chilly silence, remembering the ghost tales of the night. "Holy crap ... what the ...?" someone mumbled. I knew it wasn't just me. The little girl ghost harmed no one, but there she was in the photo, hovering over our scrum.

A couple of the nieces that were on that Ireland trip were on our farm the day we received the letter about the hidden cemeteries. It unnerved them so much that they were both up all night, fretting about bumping into a wayward ghost on their way to the bathroom. (What can I say? We have small bladders in my family.) In the morning, we all agreed that we should just let the cemeteries sit undisturbed. Why tempt the spirits?

I think about those 24 people when I walk the property now. I believe that some spirits get stuck between this world and the next. But I don't want to bump into one on our farm, in my house, or anywhere else. And I certainly don't want to annoy any of them by moving their resting places around.

So instead of letting people root around in old graves, I tell the pre-Civil War folks to rest well. And to stay right where they are. Right. There.

Hope they like what we've done with the place.

Middle of the Road

My husband, "Farmer Brown," and I had the mile-long gravel road on our farm blacktopped. After looking at the costs involved in repeatedly replacing and spreading the gravel several times a year, coupled with the enormous amount of our farm manager's time and energy to do so, we decided that blacktopping the road was a worthwhile investment.

It's a beauty. The new road weaves its way from the front gate of the farm; past two barns; two homes (those of our farm manager, Mark, and his father); a garage; and several fields of bucolic pastureland full of happy, contented horses. Driving on our gleaming, new blacktop road I think of the distinctly American penchant for road trips—taking off in a car, heading west or south or wherever to clear one's mind, rolling down the windows, cranking up the tunes. It's the stuff of which car commercials, movies, and novels are made.

While I also have romantic notions of road tripping, I have a bad history of leaving a little too much of myself behind on trips. All throughout my youth, I would get motion sickness and end up puking on car trips. I puked on the way to and from West Virginia every summer. I puked on the way home from Cedar Point Amusement Park every summer. (Thank you, Tilt-a-Whirl, or rather, "Tilt-a-Hurl."). I puked in the back of the tour bus on Big Sur in California, and my two older brothers had to clean it up. I puked into my mother's purse on a bus during a family trip to Ireland (giving new meaning to "the wearing of the green").

Even now, when I am traveling by bus or car, I insist on sitting up front, popping anti-nausea medication, and donning those goofy acupressure wristbands so that I can keep an eye on the horizon.

My dad used to have a motorhome when I was little, and he would take my brothers on excellent adventures out west to see places like the Grand Tetons, Yellowstone, and the Grand Canyon. I was so envious of their stories of camping, getting lost, and seeing amazing sights. But I never got invited. I guess between my hurling and my bedwetting, I wasn't a desirable travel companion. I would love to have seen my father, a sensible man who lived in wingtip shoes, "roughing it" with a bunch of knucklehead young men in close quarters, squeezing his 6'4" frame into that motorhome's lilliputian-sized bathroom.

When I was a stay-at-home mom, I would occasionally get an irrational urge to hit the road. Those were challenging years. I had three little girls who had various issues (eating disorders, learning disabilities, dietary allergies, anxiety, power struggles, math homework, mean girl drama). My entrepreneurial husband worked crazy long hours. And my mother was slowly succumbing to Alzheimer's. Out running errands, alone on I-90, with nothing but the road in front of me … I would fantasize about blowing past my exit and heading west to California to … I don't know. Reinvent myself by becoming a soap opera actress, taking up surfing, or maybe getting some sleep? "See ya, suckas!" I would say in my imagination, flipping my finger through the car's moonroof. But, of course, that never actually happened.

I took a road trip with my daughters to bring our youngest back to school in Maine. It was a 14-hour drive, so we decided to break it up into two days. The first day we stopped at a kooky little place in New York called Lily Dale. It was kind of a mystic version of Chautauqua (a cultural retreat also in New York). We heard that every year since 1879, droves of people descended upon this little village—that reportedly was in a vortex of some kind—to commune with spirits, contact dead relatives, and have revelations. Turns out, after spending a fortune on parking and lunch, we didn't get much. We went to a free group "reading" in the woods where a panel of mystics read the crowd … and we got what we paid for … a whole lot of vague generalities.

"I'm getting something for an Ann. Is there an Ann in the crowd?" Silence. "No … not Ann … Mary. Is there a Mary here?" (Well, hell, of course there's a Mary or an Ann in the crowd full of women aged 50+. Doesn't take a clairvoyant to figure that out.)

One of the mystics asked if a woman had any connection to Bob Seger. When she shook her head "no," the mystic pressed on. "Did your person ride a motorcycle?" No. "Is his name Bob? Robert?" No. "Did he wear a leather jacket?" No. "Are you sure his name isn't Bob?" No. "Well, I'm still getting Bob Seger," she insisted as she moved on, as if this poor woman was either lying or slow.

The rest of that road trip was like a sing-along, a therapy session, and a mom-and-daughter date all rolled into one. We had two cars, so I took turns with different combinations of daughters. Ginny and I sang songs from *Hamilton* and *The Drowsy Chaperone*. Grace and I sang favorites from Feist and the Killers. Rose and I listened to podcasts; talked about plans for the future and politics; and recounted our ridiculous Lily Dale visit. It was worth the sore back and frozen hips I got by the end of fourteen hours in the car to have extended time with my girls who are now scattered to the wind, traveling their own roads, finding their own adventures.

These days, I keep thinking of that great Pretenders song, "Middle of the Road." Chrissie Hynde says, "I'm standing in the middle of life, with my plans behind me … I'm not the cat I used to be. I got a kid, I'm thirty-three." I'm in my 50s, and many of my plans are behind me. But with Alzheimer's disease back in my life ravaging my mother-in-law and sister, I'm all about finding joy where I can. I'm looking at the road in front of me, fighting back an uncharacteristically manic drive to do it all now. But I'm also enjoying the ride as I meditate each morning with my new mantra, "Seize the day, mothafucka," relishing walking on a newly paved blacktop road through a gorgeous stand of tall trees, listening to the wind through the leaves, and counting the blessings that got me to the middle of this road.

Game Rooms

"I'm setting up the basement of the farmhouse as a game room," I said.

"Great idea!" my husband replied. "That's going to be so cool."

I never thought of him as being all that enthusiastic about board games. But I proceeded to bring all the games down to the basement: Scrabble, Bananagrams, Boggle, Uno, Chutes & Ladders (or as I call it, Purgatory), playing cards, and even a ping-pong table. "It will be nice to have rainy day group activities for folks who come down to visit," I thought.

Shortly after that, my family and I traveled to the Montreal Jazz Festival in Canada. My husband and I had attended the festival a few times before and wanted to share it with our girls.

It is a nonstop musical celebration with incredible musicians from all over the world. And Montreal is an amazing city; it feels like you're in Europe but without the jet lag.

We were all very excited to explore the city when my husband went rogue, as is his wont. "I've booked a date with Musky Mike. I'm going musky fishing," he declared. "Anyone want to join me?"

Silence. We had come all this way to one of the great cities of North America, full of beautiful architecture, great food, and of course, world renowned music at the jazz festival … no one was interested in hanging out with Musky Mike on a cold river when we could be drinking café au lait or wine in the city.

The girls and I dawdled around Montreal, touring churches, galleries, and local restaurants. When we met up with my husband, Musky Mike's new best friend, later that day, he was ebullient. "You should see this fish! We were in about three feet of water, and Musky Mike told me just what to do. It took me about a half hour to get him in, but I landed a huge musky." And he did. The fish weighed about 35 pounds and stretched about 52 inches. He could not stop looking at the photo of his epic catch, showing it to friends and strangers alike. This went on literally for years. Sometimes, even today, I will find him gazing lovingly at the image on his phone … over 10 years later.

"I'm going to have a replica made and hang it in the game room at the farm," he gushed.

"Well … we'll see," I cautioned.

"But that's what a game room is for … for showing off your kills. This musky is just the beginning," he replied.

It dawned on me that for the past year we were each talking about different "game." Me: Parcheesi; him: dead animals.

You see, my husband has long had game room envy. Our farm neighbors, Eric and Judy, have an epic game room, or more appropriately, a trophy room. Some might call it a room of death. Eric is an avid, accomplished hunter and has traveled all over the world hunting bears, antelopes, wildebeests, crocodiles, and of course, good old Ohio deer. And each of these kills has a place in his game room. He has complete reverence for each of his conquests and thrilling stories of how he got them. Judy is much quieter about it all, almost apologetic about the still life display of once animated subjects. "I should be named Wife of the Year, honestly," she says as she gently picks dust fuzzies from the bear.

So, we now have a very realistic musky hanging in our game room, all by itself, over by the pool towels. I'm hoping he doesn't get company any time soon, but my husband is threatening to hang a big deer head down there when he lands one.

Now, I've got nothing against hunters, really. Eric has schooled me plenty on how hunting is actually good for animals: it controls the animal population (which, hello, is much needed here with Ohio deer). And in African villages, it offers jobs and local income for guides, permits, vehicles, etc. as well as food for the locals. It also discourages poaching, which is a completely heinous, immoral act.

But I sincerely don't want to be met with an animal head hanging on my wall. I was afraid of my parents' painting of the Sacred Heart of Jesus, for goodness sake. As a child, Jesus' eyes followed me all over the room. I can only imagine how Mr. Deer will freak me out.

But I know I'm going to lose this fight. Musky Mike's BFF will eventually become "The Deerslayer" one of these days. He says he's waiting for "the big one" with a giant rack.

I guess maybe I can hang my pool towels on its antlers.

Slacking Sluggers

For the past thirty-one years since college graduation, my Marquette University friends and I have gotten together each fall to spend some time at a cabin on a quiet lake in northern Minnesota.

When we were new college graduates, the weekends up there were brief, beer soaked and silly—full of music and dancing. Over the years, our gatherings turned into veritable therapy sessions talking about jobs, husbands, partners, kids, dogs, heartbreak, aging parents, parents gone, dreams deferred, worry, regret … life.

We dubbed our weekends together "Slugfest," as in lying around like slugs. As life got busier and more complicated, these weekends away with each other became a beacon, a goal. We always told each other to "just hang on until Slugfest."

We do crossword puzzles as a team (the only way I have been able to complete one) and play Chinese checkers. Our beverages have gone from cheap beer to gourmet coffee and good wine. And our menus have progressed from potato chips and pizza to downright fine dining. One year, early on, our conversation at dinner drifted to talking about appliances and I remember saying, "Wow, we must really be adults now. This is so boring."

When my husband and I had the good fortune to become farm owners, I immediately thought, "This would be a great clubhouse for the Sluggers!" By then, we Sluggers were all turning 50 and decided that life was too short for just one Slugfest a year. We deserved two: a Lake Slug and a Farm Slug. And so, the Sluggers migrated south from Minnesota, where they all live, to Ohio.

As the Sluggers arrived at the farm and unpacked their bags, I made a fire in the fireplace, eager to get down to slugging. Then, my friend, Sheila, unpacked a special gift for me: a slackline. "Does this mean we have to get off the couch?" I said, putting it on the bar and pouring myself a drink.

For those who are older than thirty, a slack line is a hipster device that is essentially a wide tight rope that one installs between two trees and then, if one is an agile twenty-something, one tiptoes across with ease and grace. Sheila decided that, while she valued our penchant for lying around, she thought we all needed a challenge. She had triplets who were teenagers, so she was clearly sleep deprived and not thinking straight. I, being a good hostess, begrudgingly agreed to help get it set up later, hoping she would forget about it.

Unfortunately for me, she remembered the slack line the day after a particularly festive evening of dancing and revelry. Sheila was insistent on getting that slack line up. Eager to shake the cobwebs off my brain, I jumped in … or rather shuffled. The other two ladies there, Maura and Michelle, looked on and sipped coffee as Sheila and I wrestled, grunted, groaned, and were generally stymied by the slack line. We were down on all fours for hours, twisting the line, turning it this way and that, swearing like sailors. The instructions were incomprehensible, so we Googled for better directions. Instead, we found some videos of hilariously douchey dudes assuring viewers that slack lines were amazing for "amping up your workout" and "really challenging your abs, dude!"

"Oh, for chrissake," I thought. "Can't we just get a Bloody Mary and call it a day?"

We persevered, albeit clumsily, with more swearing and grunting. When we finally, miraculously had the blasted thing up, we both let out ecstatic, almost obscene sounds like that famous scene from *When Harry Met Sally*—"Yes! Yes! Yes!"—collapsing on the ground in delirious laughter. The horses nearby rolled their eyes, swinging their tails at flies as the four of us immediately went inside for a nap.

The slack line remained between two trees outside our farmhouse for a few weeks after The Sluggers' departure. My daughters and I gave it a few runs. My husband kept threatening to try it but never got around to it. It now sits under the deck, waiting for the Sluggers' return visit.

We don't talk much between our gatherings, preferring to save it all up for those magical weekends where time stands still and we are almost back in college, only now with wrinkles and sensible shoes.

Badass Barn Cat

When I was little, the most beautiful girl in third grade, Barbara Vanderbilt, had a cat that had kittens and for some reason, she bestowed one on me. I humbly accepted this honor, secretly hoping that some of Barbara's blonde-haired, blue-eyed beauty would miraculously transfer to me through her kitten. I remember Barbara as a tiny third-grade version of Brigitte Bardot. I was a chubby, slightly stinky, perpetually stuffy-nosed kid with dirty ankles and what my mother lovingly referred to as "dishwater blonde" hair. I went up against Barbara for the coveted part of Dolly in our class' rendition of *Hello Dolly* at Monsignor Weygand's Jubilee Celebration, but who was I kidding? I couldn't hold a candle to Barbara's star power. Barbara nailed it with effortless aplomb.

Anyway, I accepted Barbara's kitten and brought it home, much to my mother's surprise. The kitten was light orange, the color of cheese crackers, so I named her Crackers. I loved her so much, but neither my mom nor I knew a damn thing about kittens or how to raise them. My mother was way too busy with a houseful of teenage boys and their friends, 24/7, to read up on the care and keeping of kittens. Needless to say, our life was a little too hectic for poor Crackers. A few days into her stay with us, Crackers went missing, and no one could find her. I was bereft until one of my brothers opened the refrigerator and there was Crackers, hanging from the egg rack on the door. She was alive, but pretty chilly.

Crackers ran away the next day. I can't blame her. She figured she'd take her chances out in the wild. It couldn't be more dangerous than our chaotic house—and our fridge.

When we acquired our farm, I was delighted to find that it came complete with two cats—and they were orange, just like Crackers.

These cats are working cats, cold-hearted killers. It is their job to keep mice and other varmints out of the barns, and these felines are fierce.

Hell, they've been at it for over 30 years (yes, really). Something about the country air seems to be good for these guys' vitality, in spite of their dangerous lifestyles. They are named Tom and Jerry, though I'm still not sure which is which. One, let's say it's Jerry, we call "The Pet Sematary Cat" because he looks like he's back from the dead. He has survived several brushes with death, including being run over by a tractor. He walks, or rather, lumbers in a sideways fashion, kind of like John Wayne, and seems to be mumbling to himself all the time, "Don't say it's a fine morning or I'll shoot ya."

Jerry is always friendly though, coming out of nowhere to greet whoever enters the barn, rubbing up against our legs. But make no mistake; he's a killing machine. As our farm manager, Mark says, "No mouse, rat, chipmunk, or small rabbit is safe under his watchful gaze." His one ear is mangled; he has many lumpy tumorous protrusions on his belly. But he's been showing up for work every day for the past 30+ years, ready to kick some ass and take no prisoners.

Our dog, Taj Mahal, has a healthy respect for Jerry. They pretty much agree to disagree. Taj darts into the barn; Jerry moves into the shadows or the corners of an empty stall. Taj tiptoes up to him, and Jerry stares him down, "Bring it on, you filthy mongrel."

Taj creeps closer. The cat lets out a hiss, and my 80-pound Doberman takes off the other way, "Sorry! I thought you were someone else!" Taj gets his revenge eventually, though, as he runs over to Jerry's food bowl and snarfs the entire thing in seconds flat, cautiously watching Jerry with a side-eye as he does so.

Jerry just rolls his eyes and lumbers away, "Whatever, dude. Just watch your back."

A Pet Bait and Switch

My daughter, Ginny, and I were taking in the warm spring air
down on the farm whilst brewing in the hot tub when we noticed a
very busy bluebird couple setting up house in a birdhouse nearby.
It was mesmerizing. Mr. Bluebird was warily eyeballing us from a
tree branch as he dove in and out. Granted, we were hard to see,
what with our camo bathing suits. Eventually, he decided we were
harmless, swooped in with a beak full of something, and lighted just
outside of the doorway of the birdhouse. Pretty soon, Mrs. Bluebird
did the same. We were rapt in attention. In and out they went,
dutifully caring for a house full of hungry beaks. When we strained to
listen, we could just barely hear the baby bluebirds' tiny little peep-
peeps as they hungrily devoured their meals.

"This is the way to have pet birds," I thought. "Outside. Just like
those barn cats."

My mind went back to the pet birds from my past. Pets never lasted
long in my house growing up. But there was a time around the mid-
'70s when my parents were all about canaries. My dad had always
wanted a canary. So we owned two different canaries: Bing (as in Bing
Crosby, the crooner) and Twitty (as in Conway Twitty, the country
music star). They were lovely—small and yellow with beautiful songs.

I'm not sure how those birds survived in a hectic house full of people
in and out at all hours. One of the canaries did meet a tragic end
while I was out of town with my parents. Twitty mysteriously kicked
the seed bucket while under the care of my older brothers. The details
are murky, but it involved a microwave.

Fast forward to when I myself was a young parent with three eager,
animal-loving children. It was decided that, okay, we would get
a gerbil. (God help me. Aren't gerbils just a hair away from being
mice?) My husband, "Dr. Doolittle," an animal lover himself, took the
girls to the pet store to pick one out. Next thing I knew, my husband

and posse were walking in the door with a very large cage containing a feathered friend, a cockatiel. She was very beautiful, I must say. All yellow and white with bright red circles on her cheeks, like hastily applied rouge.

"A bird?! What happened to the gerbil?!" I exclaimed as they excitedly paraded our new pet into the kitchen.

"Oh, we just thought this bird was so pretty," my husband replied. "And look, she jumps right onto my finger."

The girls ingeniously named our new pet bird Polly.

So, there I was with three little girls and a brand-new pet bird. All was well and good for the first three years or so. The girls would watch TV or play house with the bird. Our youngest, Rose, loved setting up doll play villages in the basement where Polly the bird would rampage through the town, nibbling on the dolls and charmingly pooping all over Main Street like an incontinent Godzilla.

"Dr. Doolittle," a world-class whistler, taught Polly how to sing the theme song from *The Andy Griffith Show*. They were quite a team, like Edgar Bergen and Charlie McCarthy. They entertained adults and children alike at dinner parties. But Polly never really took a shine to me.

"That Andy Griffith number is wearing a little thin," I thought one day. "She needs new material." So, I tried to teach her "Whistle While You Work" from *Snow White*. It seemed like a perfect ditty for her. Nothing. Day after day, month after month, I would whistle to her, but that damned bird just stared at me in defiance. "Come on, you filthy animal, sing the bloody tune," I would growl at her. Still, nothing.

About five years into our relationship, Polly took an evil turn. We got a very large, 100 lb. Doberman Pinscher, and that bird tortured the dog every day. She would sneak over to the dog's cage and light on top of it, pooping on top of the dog in an impressive display of the pecking order. She would wander over to the dog's hubcap-sized water bowl and take a bath in it. The indignity of it made our Doberman beyond neurotic. And then there was the screeching. We had old, funky kitchen drawers that would stick and screech when we would open and close them, and Polly began to imitate that sound.

"Really? You'll imitate that obnoxious sound and won't cough up a 'Whistle While You Work?' That's fucked up," I would whisper to her. "You are a mean-spirited little bugger."

It continued like that for another couple of years. Polly would scream and make the most annoying racket all day until Rose walked into the room. After all, they had spent many quality hours in those doll villages together. When Rose was around, Polly would break into that damned Andy Griffith song, trilling away with unbounded joy. It was torturous. What the hell was the matter with that damned bird?

We had to take Polly to the vet every month or so to keep her wings clipped, else she fly all over the house, which was almost as irritating as her screeching. To make matters worse, Polly was afraid of heights, so if she would fly up to the top shelf of a bookcase, for instance, she would panic and screech to the rafters until one of us retrieved her.

At her monthly wing-trimming appointment, I asked the vet about Polly's incessant screeching and fixation on my youngest daughter. "Oh, that's typical in adolescent male birds," he exclaimed. "He's probably attached to your daughter and thinks she is a bird, like him. He's flirting."

"Um … wait," I replied. "Polly is a dude?"

"Yep, and he's got a crush on your daughter," the vet reiterated.

To get away from the racket, and to make room for the Holy Spirit between the bird and my daughter, I began to put "Pauli" (spelling adjusted for his newly discovered gender) outside in his cage. On one such occasion, we forgot about the bird and mistakenly left him outside overnight. A raccoon tried to break into his cage and knocked it off the patio table, damaging the door; it never really closed tightly thereafter.

A few days later, I came zooming home after running errands— just in time to get the kids off the bus. As I jumped out of my car, I noticed that familiar, grating sound. Just then, my daughter, Ginny, got home from the bus stop. She heard it too. We both followed the sound into the backyard where we found Pauli on top of his cage, screeching to high heaven. "Oh crap," I thought. "This is not going to end well."

The two of us slowly tiptoed toward the bird, trying to coax him onto my finger. Then, in another act of defiance toward me, as if to say, "Screw you, lady!" off he flew into the bushes nearby. Ginny and I closed in on him and were just about to grab him when he flew—first to the top of the bush, then to the top of a 200-foot-high monster oak tree. "Oh, for God's sake. You stupid motherlovingsonofabitch asshole bird," I muttered aloud. There he was, at the top of the tallest tree in town, afraid of heights and unable to figure out how to fly down to us like a, you know, bird.

Pauli's lover, my daughter Rose, was completely bereft, inconsolable. We each tried to talk him down, but it was no use. That stupid, infuriating bird stayed at the top of that tree for three full days. It was especially heinous—torturing my daughters with his proximity but with no earthly way to retrieve him. I was out of my mind.

"Oh for God's sake, you stupid idiot! You need to either die or fly. This is ridiculous. We cannot do this for one minute longer," I silently begged. And so, he flew. Finally. We told the girls he flew to Florida, but honestly, I hope he flew to the jaws of Hell, that little bastard.

Poor Rose mourned his loss for months, and that just ate me up. But I'm not going to lie, I didn't miss him. Still don't. We had him for nine years … which was eight years too many. But I got off easy. Those buggers live to be 25-years-old.

So, no more birds as pets for me. I'll stick to admiring them in the wild, where birds don't sing theme songs, aren't afraid of heights, and don't put the moves on my daughter.

The Gadget Queen

One of my favorite discoveries in the region of our farm property is an Amish country store named Lehman's Market. "Country store" belies the enormity of this place. It's more like an Amish Mall of America. This sprawling entity includes everything a good Amish household might need. The hardware section is a walk back through time with potbelly stoves; axes for cutting firewood; and all manner of wrenches, hammers, and manly old-timey devices. Then there's the kitchen section—row upon row of accoutrements, large and small. Materials for making, storing, carrying, serving one's own bread, pasta, jam, cakes, pies, soups, stews, stocks … stuff that would make Julia Child drool. It is this department that I just had to bring my best friend to see on a cold, dreary winter day.

My friend, Kammy, is a wonderful cook and she loves kitchen paraphernalia. She putters endlessly around her kitchen, using her special gadgets meant for anything imaginable. Juicing a small lemon? Got the gadget. A large lemon? Got a different gadget. Observing her in her kitchen, she's forever picking every last bit of beef off the bone so she can make it into a soup or stew later. She is constantly cooking, storing, and freezing food, ready to put on a gorgeous buffet at a moment's notice. Once, when she hosted my sisters and me for a weekend at her lake home, she disappeared for a few moments and was chatting with us from the other room. We barely knew she was gone before she somehow magically returned with freshly made ice cream (she's got a gadget for that too) and a peach pie that made us weep with joy.

She comes by her cooking prowess naturally. Kammy's mother is a Hungarian immigrant. She and her sister were raised by their Hungarian grandmother and great aunts, and all the recipes and traditions that came with them. I grew up across the street from Kammy, and going into her house as a child was a cultural adventure. The house was subdued, bathed in a late '60s glow of burnt oranges, pinks, and goldenrod yellows. The Hungarian aunties were always in the kitchen, stirring bubbling pots on the stove, steam rising, enveloping their babushkas in mystery. There were smells there that I never found in my own mother's kitchen: paprika, roasted peppers, goulash, stews, soups, noodles slathered in something amazing and foreign (probably just butter, but it smelled different there). Their Hungarian chatter, reprimanding us as we wandered through the room with Barbies in tow, was both exotic and familiar.

As a teenager, Kammy enlisted her aunties' help to tackle the painstaking task of making a Hungarian Dobos Torte: a multi-layered, complicated Hungarian delicacy that took her probably two days to make. I remember thinking, "Why would you do that when you could just crack open a perfectly good Sarah Lee pound cake and have at it?" But Kammy persevered, creating a lovely, delicate pastry that would make any bakery envious. Tragically, it ended up in a heap, when, while it was setting up in the basement, a load of laundry came down the shoot and blew it to smithereens.

As I remember Kammy's kitchen, I hear Hungarian chatter and the aunties' silhouettes morph into my friend at present day, pecking through the kitchen aisle at Lehman's, looking for just the right spatula; there are maybe twenty varieties there. I chuckle to myself, looking at her, knowing her culinary traditions and comparing it to my own meat-and-potatoes upbringing.

My mother's kitchen door was always open, ready to feed whomever happened to walk through. It wasn't fussy food—no desserts that took half a week to prepare—but it was the epitome of comfort food. That kitchen was chaotic and improvisational. My mother liked to cook ... enough. It was a necessary part of the job description. Everything was made in large quantities. There was usually an overcooked chicken grilled out in the nice weather plus eye of round and a mountain of mashed potatoes on Sundays. The smoke alarm would go off when the oven door was opened to reveal charred dinner rolls. (I was routinely enlisted to scrape the blackened bottoms off those dinner rolls.) I don't remember salad showing up in that kitchen until the mid-'80s. Kammy grew up in my mom's kitchen probably as much as she did in her own. She spent many, many hours with me in our kitchen peeling potatoes, setting the table, eating, clearing the table, doing the dishes, sweeping the floor, feeding a baby nephew or niece at my mother's expansive kitchen table.

Entering my farm kitchen from our sojourn to Lehman's, Kammy and I unpack our booty of fine cast iron pans, an apple peeler gizmo, a nifty dish soap dispenser, and a tiny yellow whisk with a duckling on the handle. Once we cure the pans, we fall into a familiar rhythm of chatting, sipping wine, passing the olive oil to saute the onions, preparing a steak for the grill. And then she reaches down into my spice drawer for the Hungarian paprika, sprinkling it liberally. The scent memory takes me back to those aunties, the goulash, and all those times spent in the kitchens over the years.

Water Signs

According to soothsayers, my astrological chart is "loaded with water." I am a Cancer, which is a water sign, and I'm married to an Aquarius, "the water bearer." I've been told I will always be around water, surrounded by it, even if that means having leaky pipes. So, it makes perfect sense that our farm is situated right on top of a huge, underground aquifer. Turns out this part of Ohio is loaded with water in the form of rivers, streams, lakes, and aquifers.

I grew up near Lake Erie—still live close to it now—and love looking out over the water, even just seeing it as I drive by. (Those who have never seen a Great Lake have no idea how impressive they are.) But I never thought I would have a home on top of a hidden lake.

Being surrounded by water comes in handy because I'm pretty sure my husband is a merman. It first occurred to me way back when we went to Australia in winter for our honeymoon. One of our stops was an island on the Great Barrier Reef. He couldn't wait to get into the ocean there, and once he was in, I couldn't get him out. I was journaling under a palm tree, watching him slowly cruise and poke around in the shallow water until he emerged, breathlessly telling me that he saw more variety of fish snorkeling in chest-deep water than he had in all his scuba dives combined. He begged me to join him in his scuba diving adventure the next day. Giddy with newlywed loyalty, I forced myself to do it. I took the resort course the next day, which pretty much taught me how not to kill myself and, the cardinal rule of diving, "Stick with your buddy."

The next thing I knew, we were 60 feet deep in the clear, azure waters of the Reef for two dives.

The first dive is a blurry memory of me concentrating on staying alive. I had learned in my resort course how to retrieve my mask and regulator if either of them became dislodged, but had quickly decided they were staying put, thank you very much. I spent the entire time checking the water for great white sharks, holding my regulator tight against my mouth, and pressing my mask even tighter against my face.

On the way to our second dive, I sucked in the surface air and thanked God I was still alive. The first mate tied up the boat to a buoy, we all ate lunch, and we prepared ourselves for the next dive at a famous site called the "Cod Hole."

The boat began to rise and fall with the ocean swells, and I slowly turned more and more green, eyes fixed on the horizon, trying to talk myself out of heaving my guts over the side of the boat. Just then, my husband ("The Merman") called out, "Hey captain! It looks like we've got company." Everyone froze and followed his gaze over the water. There, about fifty yards from the boat, jutting out of the water, were two enormous dorsal fins … sharks.

"Well, that's just perfect," I thought to myself. The first mate—a daredevil, redheaded Aussie—jumped into a Zodiac dinghy and raced over to the dorsal fins. Everyone on the boat stood in tense silence as the Aussie kicked at the sharks. "What in the hell is he doing?" I thought. "I am going to watch this lunatic get eaten alive." But inside I was relieved. "Well, we're clearly going in to shore," I thought. "Nothing ruins a tourist dive more than the first mate being turned into chum."

The Aussie returned to the boat, however, and declared, "They're just a couple of tiger sharks, about four meters each, chomping on some whale blubber that's stuck to the reef." (I did some quick math … holy mackerel, that was thirteen feet!) As I started to take my gear off and open a beer to celebrate the end of our diving adventure, he shouted, "But, they're not frenzyin' … we're going in!"

"What the?! Excuse me?" My knees went out from under me, and I'm pretty sure I shat myself.

My husband immediately suited up, went to the back of the boat, and caught my tearful stare. "Babe … you don't have to do this if you don't want to …." And then, splash! He was in.

All the other divers tiptoed over to the side of the boat to see if the sharks would eat my newlywed husband. As he slowly descended beneath his bubbles, one by one, the divers on board joined him in the water. I was the last one standing, blubbering alone on the deck, struggling with a mix of seasickness and fear. "Oh, screw it," I finally said to myself. "I think I'd rather be eaten by a tiger shark than feel this lousy for one more minute."

Into the water I went. All alone in the middle of the water column, I fought back my fear, nausea, and panic. I slowly descended the 60 feet to meet my group. I could see them below, surrounded by enormous grouper, or as the Aussies call them, "potato cod". "I'll just land on that large rock below and survey the scene from there," I thought. Except that the large rock turned out to be a very large grouper who was not at all pleased with my tickling his backside with my flippers. I careened away from him, crashing into a stack of exquisite staghorn coral, sending it into smithereens. I caught the eye of the divemaster through a veil of bubbles; he just shook his head at me in disgust.

The dive proceeded through veritable canyons of vibrant coral and a variety of amazingly beautiful fish. Occasionally I would lose track of my husband and scream at him through my regulator into the ocean, "Stick with your buddy!" followed by a variety of choice expletives, only to discover he was floating above me the whole time, blissfully at home in his natural state.

I spent the entire next day on a lounge chair, drinking mimosas with a Japanese woman named Mayumi who spoke exactly zero English while my new husband went on more dives without me.

A year later, I got my scuba diving certification. I figured if we were going to be doing more scuba diving in our marriage, I needed to know what the hell I was doing. And indeed, we have had many wonderful (and a few terrifying) dives since.

So, all these years later, we have a farm on top of a lake. We do have a swimming pool, too. And, just to make sure my merman husband is okay, we made it a saltwater pool. Sharks not included.

Grown-up Sleepovers

When I was very young, the idea of a sleepover terrified me. It wasn't the spooky stories that I knew were part of the package, or even the wrath of my father, who strictly forbade sleepovers, but the fact that I was a bedwetter. No one but my very small circle of neighborhood friends knew my shameful secret. Every night, without fail, after worrying about demons, bears, a nuclear holocaust, and my parents dying before morning, I would finally fall into a deep, deep sleep. So deep that nothing was waking me. Not the constant snore of my dad across the hall; not Prince Charming's kiss; and never, never the urge to leave the warm, safe island of my bed, brave the hot lava of the floor, and make my way across the hall to go to the bathroom. The only thing that woke me was the discomforting wake-up call of chilly, damp sheets. Groggy and cold, I would rise, put on dry clothes, throw a towel on the bed, and blearily fall back to sleep. And that was only sometimes. Mostly, I'd sleep right on through 'till morning, waking up well rested and soggy.

But after my enuresis subsided and hormones moved in, I managed to make it to a couple of "cool girl" sleepovers, only to discover that adolescent sleepovers were like psychological Russian roulette. Huddled in a basement, someone would announce something like, "Okay, let's all go around the circle and say what we don't like about Beth."

Then, one by one, like some pre-teen star chamber, they would start. "Well, Beth is funny, and nice, and really good at kickball ... but she's kind of conceited, ya know?" The circle of girls would nod knowingly, afraid to speak up, lest they fall prey to this pubescent inquisition. And then the next one would start. "Um, Beth is really pretty, but ..."

"What the hell?" I thought. "Must find an excuse to leave the circle ... I have to go to the bathroom (always). Gosh I could use another Tab cola. Who wants more potato chips? Was that my mother calling?" I was eventually in the room for the mean girl round robin as the girl in the spotlight. I looked down at the goldenrod shag carpet and swallowed hard. It began, "Mary is funny ... and nice ..." And then I may have blacked out from stress.

Fast forward to present day. I'm getting ready for friends to have an overnight stay at our farm—fluffing the bed pillows, making sure I have enough essentials on hand (wine, snacks, coffee). These overnights have nothing in common with those mean girl hazing events from my youth. These sacred nights offer uninterrupted time to rest, digest, reflect, opine, laugh, and cry with longtime girlfriends.

Different overnight groupings celebrate various stages of my life: childhood, high school, college, young motherhood, work life, time spent volunteering, family. Getting together to go out to dinner is great. But there's something singular about not having to rush, pay the restaurant bill, say your goodbyes ... it's the unhurried time together that a grown-up sleepover brings. In these precious hours, I get to really see my girlfriends. Over the comfort of a dinner prepared together, some freshly muddled cocktails or wine, we share old and new stories about ourselves, each other, our children or spouses, with maybe a little politics or celebrity gossip sprinkled in. Laughter or even a spontaneous dance party will often happen, all with slippers on, bras off. Taylor Dayne; The Go-Go's; Earth, Wind & Fire; Phil Collins; and The Cure all make appearances as we celebrate life events together.

The evenings are full of empowerment, atta-gal high fiving, Girl Boss energy, and laughing so hard I have to run to the bathroom (always).

And then ... late in the evening after the dishes are cleared and the frivolity winds down, something almost holy will happen. There, with the dog sleeping in the corner, in the dim candlelight in front of a dying fire, or outside in the summer darkness, heads tipped upwards toward the starry night, there is a feeling of utter comfort, safety. There are full bellies and full hearts that inspire an emotional trust fall into the bosom of female friendships. Things, as one good friend likes to say, get "heavy, deep, and real." Everything gets laid out on that fireplace coffee table, like sacrificial offerings on the altar of friendship.

"So ... he says he never loved me," one friend sighs out as she sips her tea. "Can you believe that shit?"

There is nothing to say, really, but I blurt out, "Rotten bastard," as I swig my wine.

There is a beat, and another friend adds, "Welp, my husband is driving me crazy, but I'm used to that. It's my son that I cannot stand. I love him, sure, but … I don't like him. He's just so … he's not a nice person. Nice mom, huh? Give me that wine bottle."

I refill her glass and look her in the eye, "You're a good mom. He's being a shit right now. This, too, shall pass." We clink glass to teacup, both hoping I am right.

"Jesus Christ, does it ever end?" another comrade offers. "When does mothering get easier? I am so tired of being worried, finding solutions, fixing my kids' lives. I know for a fact my mother did not worry this much."

I nod and chuckle, thinking of my own mother. She worried, sure. But she also had an amazing superpower of being able to escape into her room, nap it off, and reemerge able to handle anything.

There are no answers offered around this fireside altar, no magic bullets, no fixing, just open ears, open hearts, acceptance. In this grown-up sleepover, the nods around the circle are wise, knowing, supportive, brave, and thankful for this escape. I know that tomorrow we will re-emerge, able to handle anything. Or at least try.

My Culinary Evolution

Our Italian friends came to town to visit with the extended family after the death of my mother-in-law, and we brought them to our farm. It was the height of summer, mid-August, and time to pick tomatoes.

Every year I swear I'm not going to plant too many tomatoes ... and every year, I get carried away. At the nursery in early spring, I am so anxious for the warmth of summer, I lose myself. Plums, heirlooms, yellows, Big Boys, Better Boys, Early Girls, striped ... they're all so beautiful, I just can't resist. That year my mother-in-law passed, we planted 74 tomato plants. The thing about tomatoes is that once they start to ripen, you've got to start picking them and using them ASAP. And at the height of summer, they all ripen at the same time.

Luckily, I had a house full of Italians. I knew how to make sauce, but under the gaze of real, live Italians, I was very intimidated because, unlike them, I was not born cooking. Cleaning dishes was as far as my kitchen education went.

By the time I got to college, my specialty was macaroni and cheese with a can of tuna fish and some frozen peas thrown in. (Sounds disgusting now, but back then, it really hit the spot.) Several years later, as a young mother of two toddlers, I was cooking more, of course because, you know, I had to keep some humans alive. I befriended another neighborhood mom at the park and we got to talking about spaghetti dinners. She offered to give me her spaghetti sauce recipe. I was dumbfounded. Spaghetti recipe? Is she joking? You just boil water, throw the pasta in, and open a jar of Ragu. "What's the biggy?" I thought.

I was almost 30-years-old and literally had no idea that people made spaghetti sauce. At home. From scratch.

Once I met my husband, a food snob, things began to change culinarily.

Because he is a fishmonger, on one of our dates early on he made me dinner of baby coho salmon stuffed with scallops. I was impressed. A few weeks later, it was my turn to make dinner, only I didn't have a plan, let alone any food skills, and was going to "wing it" at his place. I had planned to make spaghetti but forgot to bring any ingredients. Once at his apartment, I naively thought I could concoct sauce from some ingredients there. After about a half hour of trying to doctor up a bottle of ketchup with water, garlic powder and embarrassed tears, I ended up ordering pizza.

Back in my farm kitchen, now as an adult who actually knows how to cook, the Italians and I were washing, scoring, flash cooking, cooling, and peeling all those tomatoes—starting to make sauce. We compared techniques, and it turns out, they cook a lot like I do, feeling their way, tasting as they go. A little bit of salt, a little bit of garlic, and a ton of basil, of course. The steam from the pot filled the kitchen, mixing with the Italian-English chatter. As the tomato sauce boiled and bubbled, reducing down to red gold, I surveyed the scene. It felt so very unifying, universal ... preparing a meal together. As the late Anthony Bourdain said, "You learn a lot about someone when you share a meal together."

My Italian guests were in the corner, arguing about something, arms flailing, fingertips pressed to thumbs to emphasize a point. I tried to disappear, quietly stirring my tomato sauce a bit more, turning down the heat to a low simmer. If, like the novel *Like Water for Chocolate* posits, food takes on the personalities and emotions of its chef, this sauce was going to be spicy. They resolved their conflict and came back to the task at hand: completing the spaghetti dinner. They blew my mind with the revelation that they don't reduce the sauce down to thicken, but rather, throw the pasta into the sauce, to cook the pasta and thicken the sauce, all at the same time. Ingenious!

The dinner that night was amazing. Surely, it was the Italians' expertise that made it so tasty. The red wine and the Italian accents around the table also helped. (And it turned out that the pasta had a little kick after all!) It got me thinking, what personality or emotion would my own cooking carry with it? Hopefully humor, sentimentality, and love. But sadly, also probably my salty tongue, my distaste for math (see earlier reference to measuring by pinches and handfuls), maybe my penchant to hang on to hurt too long, and my natural aversion to conflict that sometimes results in passive aggressiveness. And also, there's my tendency to be gassy.

Ah well, this meal, at least, was delicious.

Epilogue

Recently, my brother and his family were at the farm for a cookout, when he asked me how the horses keep the flies out of their eyes in the hot weather. I was explaining that they stand next to each other, head to opposite rear, and swish their tails in front of each other's eyes in wonderful symbiosis, when he shook his head at me laughing and said, "When did you learn all this stuff? A girl from the suburbs of Cleveland?" I shrugged, laughing with him, replying, "I don't know … it just kinda happened. I'm sort of a farm gal now."

Over the past several years, our mid-Ohio farm has become a place where I have tapped into the child inside me that loved digging in the dirt. I've spent a lot of time walking in the country, in the woods. I've gone to country markets and to antique stores. I've watched the sunrise over the misty valley at our farm. And when I started to chronicle my thoughts, musings, and stories, I nurtured my love for writing and brought it public through a blog.

In stepping out of my normal, expected routine all those years ago, out of my comfort zone, I have learned and am still learning so much: about nature, about farming, about myself. Of the approximately 1,532 things I didn't know that I didn't know are the following:

We owned chickens for a short spell, and chickens really do "come home to roost" (at night, in odd places like on top of tractors or inside a horse's feeding bowl) just like the saying!

You really do "make hay when the sun shines," because otherwise it gets all moldy and gross. I have learned that those little bundles of grass that I've seen dotting country fields my whole life are "round bales," which are used to feed livestock over the winter. And "silage" is fermented and stored in a silo before being used as food. The fermentation ends up giving the cows a little pleasant buzz. Also, "hay" is green and horses eat it whereas "straw" is for lining stalls.

The gestation period for a pregnant horse is 10 months, and horses do occasionally sleep lying down, but only for a bit. Because they are animals of prey, they instinctively are always ready to run away and so spend most of their time on the hoof.

"Thoroughbred horses" are indeed of pure breed and are widely used in "thoroughbred racing." "Standardbred horses" are an American horse breed best known for use in harness racing, where they either trot or pace. Thoroughbreds are much more temperamental, diva-like, and breed under the watchful eyes of owners, trainers, and specialists "live cover." Standardbreds are more people-oriented and are artificially inseminated.

Farmers—and our farm manager Mark, "The Sheriff," in particular and his right hand gal, Melinda—are the hardest working, smartest, most multi-skilled people I've ever known. They rise every morning before the sun rises (and I mean EVERY MORNING) without fail, to feed and to care for their livestock and their land. They know about inseminating, breeding, feeding, medicating, and birthing horses. They know how and when to plant, to reap, to sow. They know how to repair and maintain tractors, trucks, houses, electric fences, plumbing ... honestly, almost everything. It has been an honor and a privilege to observe and learn just a smidge of it all.

It is all very humbling, and it also gives me fabulous talking points for cocktail parties.

In moving out of my comfort zone all those years ago and into this unplanned, surprise farm life, I have inadvertently *created* a zone of comfort, for myself and my loved ones. It has brought me so many gifts, not the least of which is that I found the space, the time, and the inspiration to write all about it.

Thanks for reading.

RECIPES

Marge's Beef Vegetable Soup

My mother, Marge, was not a "foodie." She didn't "live to eat," she ate to live and cooked to keep people alive. But she loved making this soup because it was dinner in one pot, which meant less dishes, and, in her words, it made the house "smell grand." I have this recipe, written in her handwriting, framed in its original, perfectly imperfect form, scribbled on notebook paper. I make it several times a year for large family gatherings.

At my sister Susan's suggestion, I add 1 small, diced parsnip to the ingredients and a half of a cabbage, diced up. And my sister Therese likes to add sauteed mushrooms. But honestly, soup is a great way to clean out your produce drawer, so I'll take inventory there and add almost anything that looks like it's on its way out.

Ingredients
2 LBS of beef chuck, cut into small cubes
1 medium onion, chopped
1 can tomato soup
1 medium can of chopped tomatoes 2 cups chopped celery
1 chunk of green pepper, not big
2–4 garlic cloves
6 potatoes, chopped into medium sized cubes
1 bone marrow or neck bones
5 fresh carrots, chopped
½ small bag of frozen peas
½ LB of fresh Italian green beans, chopped

Directions
Start by sauteing the meat chunks,and onion just to brown the meat. Then add to a large pot of cold water (early in the morning) and simmer slowly with the rest of the ingredients for a couple of hours at least. Then, near the end, add salt and pepper to taste as well as the peas and green beans.

Don't cover! The smell is GRAND! (Marge writes.)

Marge recommends serving with "Grand Muffins in refrigerated section." But I serve with fresh rosemary bread or sourdough bread from the bakery section of the grocery store.

Sandra's Thanksgiving Stuffing

My mother-in-law Sandra was a beautiful cook and homemaker. Her Thanksgiving meals were epic, and this was her centerpiece. She claimed that what made it so good was that the herbs she used were from her own garden. I think the secret was the "1 cup of butter," but perhaps it is both … and the TLC with which it was prepared.

Note about the bread cubes: You have options here. Stale or toasted bread works best. The first option is that you can cut 1 ½ pounds of bread into cubes, place them in a large baking dish, loosely tent with foil, and let them sit overnight. You can also cut the cubes and put them in the oven, toasting them at 350°F until they are like croutons, about 15 minutes or so. Finally, you can buy the toasted bread cubes in bags from the store. It's your choice! You can also choose the size of your cubes. They can be small or larger for a more rustic stuffing. (Sandy always used a mixture of stale and fresh bread.)

I like to use different kinds of bread (usually two), like a sourdough and Italian, and mix the cubes. It provides great texture.

I have successfully made this a day ahead of time and reheated it. It's just as good! You can also use this mixture to stuff the bird if you wish.

Ingredients
24 ounces bread cubes, preferably toasted or stale
1 cup unsalted butter
3 cups diced sweet onion, roughly 2 large onions
2 cups diced celery
6 garlic cloves, minced
Pinch of kosher salt and pepper
3 tbsp. fresh sage, chopped
3 tbsp. fresh parsley, chopped
3 tbsp. fresh rosemary, chopped
2 ½ cups chicken or vegetable stock
½ to 1 teaspoon each of chopped fresh sage, parsley, and rosemary

for sprinkling

Directions

Preheat the oven to 350° F. Brush a 9x13 baking dish with melted butter, olive oil, or spray with nonstick spray. Place the bread in a large mixing bowl (this may be easier for you to stir!) or the 9x13 inch baking dish that you will bake it in.

Heat the butter in a large skillet or dutch oven over medium heat. Once melted, stir in the onion, celery, and garlic with a big pinch of salt and pepper. Cook until the onions and celery soften, about 8 to 10 minutes.

Stir in the sage, parsley, and rosemary. Cook for another minute.

Then stir in 1 cup of stock.

Pour the onion and celery mixture over the bread crumbs and toss well to coat.

In a small bowl or measuring cup, whisk the remaining 1 ½ cups of vegetable or chicken stock.

Pour the stock into the bread cubes. Stir and fold the bread cubes until thoroughly combined.

Bake the stuffing for 45 to 50 minutes, until the internal temperature registers 160° F. If the stuffing is getting too browned, you can tent it with foil.

To serve 4: Cut this recipe in half exactly and bake it in an 8x8 or 9x9 inch dish. Bake for the same amount of time.

To serve 12 to 16: Double this recipe exactly. Bake in a large baking dish, like a 10x15 roasting pan or two 9x13 baking dishes. Bake for roughly the same amount of time, or about 15 minutes longer.

Aunt Marie Conway Beirne's Irish Soda Bread

I have to be honest. Some folks don't care for Irish Soda Breads because they feel it tastes like buttered drywall that would only go down well with a shot of whiskey. But they haven't had this soda bread. It's so yummy and comforting and smells amazing while baking. Don't wait until March or St. Patrick's Day to make some!

The recipe makes two to three loaves, depending on pan size. If you're traveling, you can easily portion out each of these ingredients into little baggies and assemble them in your rental property or wherever. My cousin, Mary, makes two loaves fresh each morning on our family vacation and delivers them to two lucky family cabins every day. Absolutely heavenly served warm with a hot cup of tea. It's a great way to start the morning!

Ingredients
6 cups flour
1/2 to 3/4 cup sugar
3 tsp. baking powder
1 1/2 tsp. baking soda
1 1/2 tsp. salt
4 tbsp. butter
1 box (2 1/2 cups) raisins, soaked first in warm water and drained well. (You can soak overnight or just in the morning, but it makes a big difference to soak them!)
4 cups buttermilk
2 eggs

Directions
Preheat oven to 350° F.

Whisk eggs and buttermilk together.

Cut butter into flour or work it into the flour with your fingers, Then add the well-drained raisins into the dry ingredients.

Fold dry ingredients into the wet ingredients.

Add mixture to well-greased loaf pans, lightly dusted with flour.

Bake for 1 hour and 5 minutes (or longer).

When fresh out of the oven, brush butter over the top and some sugar, if you choose.

Serve with a stick of (even more) butter and local honey to drizzle on top of each slice.

Garden-Fresh Tomato Sauce

I am going to warn you, my kitchen looked like a crime scene the first time I did this, with red splatter on the white cabinets, running down the sides of the counters, puddling onto the floor. But boy was it worth it! The taste of tomato sauce made from garden-fresh tomatoes is life-changing, albeit messy. To streamline the process and harness the flavor of as many tomatoes as possible before they start rotting, my husband and I just make our sauce simple and freeze it. Then later, we pimp it out with onions, more garlic, or whatever. Like anything, the more you do this, the easier and more streamlined it gets. And it's so worth it!

Every time I make tomato sauce, I think of when our Italian friends visited us on the farm. They were forever snapping photos of the countryside, the animals, the Amish folks at the farmer's market, all the while squealing, "It's just like the movies!" Not that I ever take it for granted, but it made me appreciate the beauty of our farm all the more.

Ingredients
10–15 pounds of fresh tomatoes, peeled and chopped (see below)
1/4 cup olive oil
4 garlic cloves
1 generous sprig of fresh basil
Salt and pepper, to taste

Directions
Clean all your tomatoes in the sink to get any dirt or bugs off them. Then, start a large pot of water on the stove to boil, while you score the bottoms of each of the tomatoes. Some will be so ripe they are already splitting, so you can just put those into the scored bowl. Then get a large boil of ice water ready.

When the water comes to a boil, briefly submerge the tomatoes in boiling water until you see the skins start to peel (usually takes about 10 seconds tops, if you've got a nice rolling boil).

From there, drop them immediately into the bowl of ice water. Some of the skins will peel right off. I put the stubborn ones through a tomato peeler, which magically separates the skins and the seeds and gushes out red, flavorful tomato juice (but just to warn you, it's a total bitch to clean.) Just pour yourself some wine as you clean it, knowing that a tasty pasta dish awaits you in a little bit.

Put all your beautiful tomato juice into a large pot (probably the same one you just used to flash cook them). Add the olive oil to the sauce. Season with the salt and pepper to taste. And throw in your garlic as well as a big sprig of basil.

It's going to seem very watery at first, but don't worry. It will cook down! Bring to a nice boil, and then simmer … for about 4 or 5 hours, until the liquid has gone down considerably and you're left with a thicker sauce. As the liquid is cooling, use a slotted spoon to fish out the sprig of basil and the cloves of garlic. When it is completely cooled, carefully divide the sauce into quart-sized bags and freeze.

The Merman's Oysters Rockefeller

My husband is a fishmonger and has turned me into a huge fan of raw oysters. Honestly, our entire family loves slurping oysters whenever we get the chance. But for special occasions, especially New Year's Eve dinner parties, Oysters Rockefeller really kills. It's not all that difficult, except for the shucking part! (Be careful!) But it looks and tastes super fancy.

When we were newlyweds, we loved to go out to big, fancy New Year's Eve parties. But once we started having kids, we opted to host dinner parties with friends (and have been doing so ever since). It usually worked out perfectly, with the kids and their friends in the basement, dancing and watching Disney movies, while the adults cooked, drank, and danced in the kitchen. One year, however, everyone got sober quickly when my 3 children emerged from the basement with raging cases of pink eye. After a frantic call to the pediatrician and a fervent run to the pharmacy, the party and the dinner continued on successfully, but it was a heck of a way to ring in the new year.

Ingredients
24 oysters, in shell
1 tbsp. chopped onion
2 tbsp. snipped fresh parsley
1 tbsp. melted butter
Salt, black pepper, and paprika, to taste
1 cup chopped cooked spinach
1/4 cup fine dry bread crumbs
¼ cup freshly shredded parmesan cheese
½ cup cold butter, cut into teaspoon-sized bits

Directions
Preheat the oven to 450° F.

Carefully open the oyster shells with a shucking knife and place them on a rimmed baking sheet, taking care to not spill too much of the juice.

In a bowl, mix the onion, parsley, parmesan cheese, and butter. Spread over each oyster.

Sprinkle with salt, pepper, and paprika as desired.

Top each oyster with two teaspoons of spinach and then sprinkle evenly with 1/2 teaspoon of the bread crumbs. Dot each with a teaspoon of butter.

Place the baking sheet in the oven and bake at 450° F for 10 minutes or until heated through (the edges of the oysters should start to curl).

Serve hot.

Susan's Sausage Bread

My sister, Susan, loved bringing people together. Always in a hurry, this was a perfect thing for her to whip up before folks came over, or to quickly throw together and bring in the door to some family gathering. The bread, all wrapped in foil, was as warm as her hugs.

Ingredients
2 packages Pepperidge Farm Italian sausage
2 packages Pillsbury crescent rolls
1 cup shredded swiss or mozzarella cheese
2 cups shredded cheddar cheese
3 large eggs

Directions
Preheat the oven to 350° F.

Brown and drain sausage well.

Whip all three eggs, but put a little aside to brush the bread rolls later.

Combine sausage, cheeses, and eggs.

Gently remove the dough from the container. Be very careful with the seams especially. Dust the surface and rolling pin with lots of flour, then lay the dough down and gently push the seams together. Roll out to about 10 x 14 inches.

Put sausage mixture all over the dough with about 2 inches of dough showing around the perimeter.

From the end nearest you, start to roll the bread forward, tucking the ends in as you go. Pick up and put onto a cookie sheet. Two loaves can fit on one sheet.

Pinch and tuck the ragged edges of the ends of the rolls.

Baste the bread with a brush of the eggs.
Cook at 350° F for 45 minutes, then take a peek to see if it has browned up. Leave in until golden brown.

Let the bread set up outside of the oven for at least 15 minutes so it will cut nicely.

Kathy's Potato Salad

My sister, Kathy, brings the house down with her famous potato salad each summer. Because there's always a cast of thousands, she makes a veritable dumpster of it at a time, but this recipe is for a reasonably sized crowd, maybe 8 to 10 people. You'll just as soon see a toddler enjoying this dish, wiping it all over his face in ecstasy, as you will a hungry teenager, gorging on its creamy richness. The ultimate comfort food, it is perfect for everything from baby showers to funeral receptions. Not a terribly difficult recipe (because I don't do difficult), but it is time consuming!

Ingredients
3 lbs. Yukon Gold potatoes, chopped into ½" pieces
Kosher salt, to taste
1 ½ cup mayonnaise
1 small red onion, finely chopped
1 tbsp. Dijon mustard
1 tbsp. lemon juice
¼ cup chopped pickles
½ tsp. paprika
6 hard boiled eggs (4 for the salad, 2 for topping the salad)
¼ cup finely chopped chives
Freshly ground black pepper, to taste

Directions
In a large pot, cover potatoes with water and season generously with salt. Bring water to a boil and cook until potatoes are easily pierced with a knife, 12 to 15 minutes. Drain and let cool slightly.

In a large bowl, combine mayonnaise, red onion, Dijon mustard, lemon juice, pickles, and paprika. Stir until well combined. Kathy's big secret: Peel 4 of the hard boiled eggs and then squish them in your hands over the bowl. This breaks them into little pieces and distributes the yolk better than chopping.

Fold in cooked potatoes, eggs, and chives, then season with salt and pepper. Refrigerate until ready to serve. Best made a day ahead so the flavors marry. Right before serving, slice 2 hard boiled eggs and arrange on top of the salad, then sprinkle a little paprika over the whole top.

Kammy's Hungarian Paprikash (Paprikás Csirke)

Nothing reminds me of times spent in my childhood best friend's kitchen than the smell of Hungarian paprika. Kammy's grandmother and aunts were in that kitchen every day, cooking something amazing and delicious that was much more exotic than my mom's kitchen across the street.

This recipe is the epitome of their Hungarian cooking. You can prepare the dish to the point where you add the sour cream and hold it until later, and then finish it right before you are ready to serve.

One note: Kammy stores her Hungarian paprika in the freezer to keep in at its optimum flavor.

Ingredients
10-12 pieces of skin-on chicken legs and thighs
1 big onion, diced
1 large cubanelle or banana pepper, diced
2 medium sized tomatoes, diced (frozen or canned tomatoes also work),
2 tbsp. Canola oil
8 oz. sour cream
1 heaping tbsp. Hungarian paprika
1 tsp. flour
Salt and pepper, to taste

Directions
Season chicken with salt and pepper.

In a large saucepan or a Dutch oven, brown the chicken in the oil for about 5 minutes.

Take the chicken out of the pan and set aside. Add the onions to the chicken juices to deglaze the pan and continue to saute without the lid for a minute or until the onions are soft. Turn down the heat to simmer and add 1 heaping tbsp of Hungarian paprika. Mix that together, being careful not to burn the paprika.

Add the chicken pieces and any leftover juices back into the onion and paprika mixture and bring to a light boil. Salt and pepper to taste. Reduce heat to simmer and add about ¼ cup of water into the mixture to thin it out. As the chicken and vegetables continue to cook, they will release more liquid into the mix. Stir occasionally to thoroughly coat the chicken, making sure it does not come to a boil.

Sauté on low for about 45 - 60 minutes until chicken reads 165°F.

Remove the chicken pieces and set aside. Just before serving, add 1 tbsp. of flour to an 8 oz. container of sour cream and stir well with a small whisk or fork. Add the sour cream mixture to the sauce and stir continuously for about 2 minutes over medium heat to thicken.

Plate the chicken over some spaetzle, rice, noodles, or potatoes and pour the sauce over top. Serve nice and hot.

Acknowledgements

Special thanks to my Sluggers from Marquette University who were the first to witness and support the "What the Farm" blog concept. Thank you to Sheila for your editing help throughout. So grateful for the cheerleading and high fives from Maura and Michelle!

Thank you to my daughter, Grace, for your editing help and commiseration on the artistic process. Thank you to Ginny and Rose for your unflagging belief in me. Thank you to all who read my blog and gave me such beautiful feedback and encouragement!

Thank you for the moral support and encouragement from the tribe of friends for whom I am forever grateful: Kammy, Anne, Ann, Gretchen, Kathy, Judy, Zoller, Meghan, Mary Ann, Nancy, my Camino Sisters, my Salem Neighborhood sisters, and my BAYarts creative posse.

I am so grateful for the professional guidance I've received in this process! Thank you to my book coach, Eryka Parker at Lyrical Innovations for helping me formulate a vision and a path forward. Thank you to my editor Rebecca Ferlotti for her patience and kind explanations of what to keep in and what to carve out of my book. Thank you to David Blue for giving it all one final look for proof reading (just when I thought it was done! Thank you to Beth Conway of French Lamb Design for her brilliant ideas on my cover design and layout and for her insight and assistance with the whole marketing piece, scary as it is.

Thank you to our farm manager, Mark, whom I lovingly call "The Sheriff" because he is in charge and knows all things, and his wife Felicia. Without their wisdom, intelligence, and uncompromising dedication to excellence in all things on our farm, none of these stories would be possible.

Thank you to my friend, the late Michael Heaton, who's words, "Mary, if you can give me 60 pages, you've got a book!" Those words meant so much from such a great writer!

And thank you for the tradition of storytelling from my family of birth, my brothers, Pat, Mark, Jim, Joe, and Dan and especially the good humor, love, and wisdom from my sisters, Kathy, Therese, and our dear departed Susan.

ABOUT THE AUTHOR

Mary Conway Sullivan, a humorist from
Cleveland, Ohio, draws from her farm journey to
create this memoir. Beyond her roles, she infuses
her writing with honesty, humility, and a unique
blend of humor and empathy.

Made in the USA
Monee, IL
06 November 2023

45853281R00111